Susella's Legacy

Susella's Legacy

A Mother's Life Lessons to Her Daughter

SHARON TATE

WESTBOW
PRESS
A DIVISION OF THOMAS NELSON

WestBow Press books may be ordered through booksellers or by contacting:

WestBow Press
A Division of Thomas Nelson
1663 Liberty Drive
Bloomington, IN 47403
www.westbowpress.com
1-(866) 928-1240

Because of the dynamic nature of the Internet, any web addresses or links contained in this book may have changed since publication and may no longer be valid. The views expressed in this work are solely those of the author and do not necessarily reflect the views of the publisher, and the publisher hereby disclaims any responsibility for them.

Any people depicted in stock imagery provided by Thinkstock are models, and such images are being used for illustrative purposes only.

Certain stock imagery © Thinkstock.

ISBN: 978-1-4497-8866-7 (sc)
ISBN: 978-1-4497-8865-0 (hc)
ISBN: 978-1-4497-8867-4 (e)

Library of Congress Control Number: 2013904830

Printed in the United States of America.

WestBow Press rev. date: 03/27/2013

I dedicate Susella's Legacy first to God who provided me the words to write. Throughout this whole writing journey I have stood on Psalm 45:1 "…. my tongue is the pen of a ready writer."

Second, I dedicate this book to James, my husband and the love of my life. Thank you for loving Mother and Daddy. God's grace has enabled us to weather both good and bad. But through life's storms you've always been my rainbow at the end of those storms.

Contents

Chapter 11

Foreword

I feel extremely honored to write the forward to Susella's Legacy. I first met Susella Seals in February 2000, when I became pastor of First Community Church of Sparta, Tennessee, where she and her husband, Estel, were members. And, for the next six years, until Susella went home to be with her Lord, she was a very special blessing not only to me, but to everyone in the church.

In chapter 9 Susella's daughter, Sharon, explains why Susella's parents decided to give her that particular name, and what it meant to them. However, after serving as her pastor for the six years I was privileged to do so, the life I saw her live during those years suggests an entirely different meaning to her name, as spelled out by the following acrostic:

Sweet
Unassuming
Sincere
Elegant
Loving
Likeable
Appreciative

Susella never had a lot to say, but the few wise words she did speak always inferred a lot. In Proverbs chapter 25, verse 11, the Bible says, "A word fitly spoken is like apples of gold in pictures of silver." As I sat down to write this forward and began to think back on conversations I had with Susella during the years I knew her, this verse of scripture came to mind as a beautiful picture of some of the things I heard her say. So, as you read the account Sharon gives of the things she remembers her mother conveying, I believe you too will agree this verse of scripture is an appropriate description of her sayings.

The Bible tells us in the little book of James that true wisdom comes from God. It was very obvious to me, as I listened to what she expressed, that Susella's wisdom truly came from God. And, as you read this book, you too will be both blessed and challenged by her simple, homespun words of wisdom.

Rev. Donald J. Kelly
Pastor, First Community Church
Sparta, Tennessee

Prologue

My mother, Susella Hickey Seals, was not a celebrity. Once you were in the same room with her, however, you felt like you were in the presence of one. When she walked into a room, there was just something about her that made you want to watch her. Yes, she was a beautiful lady to look upon, but she had an *air* about her that made everyone feel special. Her quiet, genteel ways were like the kiss of a cool breeze on a hot summer day. A twinkle in Susella's eyes offered a hint of the humor that bubbled out in girlish giggles when least expected. And more times than not, she seemed to surprise even herself with the comical lines that she spoke, as if uttered from somewhere else. All of us who had the privilege and blessing of knowing her were convinced we knew where this somewhere else was – heaven. We all knew she did not belong to this earth. She was purely goodness and kindness sent to us as a glorious gift. And her purpose for being sent here was to show everyone how best to live life.

Susella's legacy is one to be shared with the world. Lessons can be applied whether you're a rock star, a movie star, crowned royalty, the leader of a country, or simply a parent, child, or sibling. Her words of insight are suitable for the rich, the poor, the confident, or the painfully shy. Life the world over would be rid of wars, murders would be obsolete, and we would shed only tears of joy if her lifestyle was observed and practiced.

Mother always told me she did not know what her purpose in life was, but I realized even as a young girl that I was a special person because God had loved me so much to pick this wonderful woman for my mother. I heard the stories of what she went through just to bring me into this world. By all accounts Mother was not supposed to live through a third childbirth. Her first child, a daughter, was named Linda; eighteen months later her son, Harold, was born.

Because she'd had rheumatic fever as a child Mother's heart was damaged, and even my father's family had not wanted him to marry Susella because "she probably won't live that long." So after having a girl and a boy there were no plans for any more children. But as Mother said, always correcting me when I talked about being an accident, "God had a wonderful surprise for our family." When she said this, I always felt like the most special girl on earth. I believe Mother made a sacrifice to bring me into this world so she could share her life purpose with the world.

In the following pages I want to present a way of living that provides love, peace, and joy for all who are willing to practice Susella's legacy. I have not attained total fulfillment in practical applications of Mother's adages, but I strive daily to improve. I believe I am simply the conduit or messenger and a student myself. I am convinced that if I had not been with Mother for fifty-four years, to observe and learn, I would probably be worth nothing or even dead by now. She and Daddy lived a life I wanted to experience. Love between them openly expressed and showered on anyone in their paths caused everyone to understand why they lived under a cloud of favor and contentment. This is not to say they did not live through hard times and heart breaks, for they had more than their fair share. But the way they handled daily living even during difficulties was one of grace and dignity at all times. I realized early what a unique model this couple represented to the family and every person who came in contact with them. I realize this truth even more now. Please join me on this journey of life principles.

CHAPTER 1

Genuineness

THE DEFINITION OF *GENUINE* IS devoid of any hypocrisy or pretense. All who had the privilege of knowing my mother agree she was sincere. No offense to Coca Cola, but Mother was "the real thing." I first titled this chapter "Authenticity"; but after recounting the story about our conversations, you will understand why I chose the more common word to describe the first aspect of my mother's character.

Susella was the most inexplicable genuine human being I have ever known. Although I am mightily prejudiced, I've yet to find a person who disagrees with me. Mother was completely unaffected by any praise or accolades directed at her. As I observed her over the years it was this one aspect of her character that caused me to believe undoubtedly that she was not like the rest of us. As a matter of fact, in private when I told Mother how wonderful she was, her reply was always the same, "Shhhh! Please do not say that about me. Jesus Christ was the only perfect person. Please do not say that to anyone else."

Of course, here I go telling the world. I haven't changed my mind and it is not a figment of my imagination as sometimes happens after a loved one dies and we see them in a better light. I have always viewed Mother this way, and it has, in turn, made me feel special that God chose her to be my mother.

There are four distinct parts to Mother's authenticity that I want to emphasize: conversation, dress, home, and worship. I am convinced if we could all practice the art of being real in these four areas, everything else in life would fall into place for us.

Conversation

"For in many things we offend all; if any man (*or woman*) offend not in word, the same is a perfect man (*or woman*) and able also to bridle the whole body." [italics mine] —James 3:2 (KJB).

OTHER WAS NOT CONSIDERED A 'big talker' as we say in the South. We all knew when Mother said something we could take it to the bank and earn interest. She always believed it was best to simply say what you mean and mean what you say. She never babbled like some of us do when we get nervous. She just simply smiled and when asked a question always answered succinctly. When asked to lead in prayer at church she seemed to turn immortal and shed tears--not in a showy way--but in simple humility, acknowledging the Great Power to whom she was speaking.

Mother realized I loved the written and spoken word. I enjoyed learning new words and their definitions. Once, as a small child, I ran to her excitedly with a new found word. She grinned saying she thought it was a wonderful experience to learn new words; that she hoped I always had a love of English because it was her favorite subject too. However, she stressed the importance of remembering when talking with people not to try and impress them with big words. She cautioned me that doing so could make a person feel inferior, and she and Daddy never wanted me to make anyone feel badly. She encouraged me to continue reading and studying, but to speak to others the way I would want them to speak to me. So the life principle here is this: When addressing anyone in conversation, speak simply and sincerely without great fanfare. It is not necessary to convince anyone of your intelligence through your vocabulary.

The single statement most repeated by anyone who knew Susella is that she never said a harmful word about anyone. What a powerful birthright to hand her family and peers. How can I make such a bold claim?

Included here is a story written in early 1939 by Susella Hickey and printed in her high school newsletter. Interestingly, the subject matter deals with tuberculosis, which she lost a brother to, and was diagnosed with herself several years later.

Scattered Violets
By Susella Hickey

The wind was howling around the little log cabin, the fire was flickering low in a small fire place, a dim light was burning low on a rickety table. Groans and coughs were coming from the small ramshackle bed where Dickie's sick mother lay.

Dickie was beginning to get hungry for the food was gone. He knew his mother had refused to eat because she wished to save food for him. Now, Mother was sick. She couldn't wash family washing for food anymore, and father, well, he had passed away when Dickie was only three months old. Mother told Dickie about his father many times and how he was sick all time. People thought there wasn't any cure for him because the dreadful disease, tuberculosis, was causing him to weaken fast. So when Dickie was only three months old the disease took his father from him.

Dickie was out of bed early next morning. There was no food in the house. Neither was there any medicine for Mother. She needed a proper diet and plenty of fresh air and sunshine. Perhaps if she could have these she would overcome the disease which was weakening her more and more each day.

"Mother, Mother," Dick said with a broken voice. "I'm going to find work."

"Dear, you can't find work. You are only a child. You are too small, Dick. There isn't anything you can do," Mother answered in a voice just above a whisper.

"But, but Mother, you've got to have food and medicine. Maybe I can find something to do; anyway, I'm going to try. Mother, you did say God helps those who help themselves. I'll be back soon," he said as he turned from the bedside and walked out the little cabin door.

His bare feet trotted along the dirt road. Not a sound could be heard except the lonesome pine trees. Dickie searched all day for work and at the end of day turned his face homeward very much discouraged. When he raised his head to see where he was, he was gazing at a large white house mounted upon a hill. "Maybe they need me," was his thought. He managed to brace up and walked up to the door.

The old gentleman was in need of a boy just his size to help feed the cows, pigs, chickens and do other chores. So this was the joy Dickie faced. To work for Mr. Long with cattle, pigs, chickens, just the very things of which he had dreamed.

He reached home as the sun was hiding behind the mountain which left a beautiful scene on the pine trees near the small log cabin. He ran up to the door, thrilled to think he could buy food and medicine for his mother. Now she would get well. Poor Mother, she has always labored so hard for me. Now I'll pay her back.

He entered the room in a rush. "Mother, Mother." There was no answer. The joy that filled Dickie's heart then *turned to fright. He walked slowly to the shabby bed and placed a small hand upon the white forehead, cold, cold.*

Dickie did not go to work for Mr. Long next day. But instead he stood over a fresh pile of clay dirt, with tears streaming from his sky blue eyes to the ground below, and watched them lower his mother in the ground. This was the saddest experience Dickie had ever faced. He scattered a few violets he had gathered which grew under the pines upon his mother's grave. With tears in his eyes and a pain in his heart he said "Goodbye Mother, dear," turned and slowly walked away.

Perhaps Dickie's mother would have recovered if she had only known in time the disease which caused her husband's death was affecting her.

[Printed beside Susella's story was this announcement:

Miss SusElla Hickey, daughter of Mr. and Mrs. J. R. Hickey of Fredonia, and Estel Seals, son of Mr. and Mrs. James Seals of Cagle, were united into the holy bond of wedlock Saturday, April 8, at the home of Mr. and Mrs. B. T. Hickey. Mr. Hickey was in charge of the ceremony.

The wedding was quite a surprise to their many friends and relatives. Mrs. Seals is a junior of S.C.H.S. and is very active in church and social affairs of her community. They will make their home at Fredonia.

Their friends take this opportunity to extend to them their best wishes for a happy married career.]

Dress

"Whose adorning let it not be that outward adorning of plaiting
the hair and of wearing of gold, or of putting on of apparel;
But let it be the hidden man (*woman*) of the heart, in that
which is not corruptible, even the ornament of a meek and
quiet spirit, which is in the sight of God of great price."
—I Peter 3: 3, 4 (KJB).

To look at Mother's appearance you would think she spent
lots of money on clothes, but in truth she did not. She told me
that during the early years of their marriage she and Daddy had it
rough financially, and living in rural Appalachian South during the
Depression was a constant struggle. Mother was forced to make her own
clothes because she couldn't afford to buy "store bought" ones.

Mother was a talented seamstress. She could design and assemble a
dress without using a pattern, a talent that never ceased to amaze me.
When I was planning my wedding, she took me shopping for a dress,
and of course the one I loved the most was too expensive for our budget.
After a full day of shopping, she suggested we return to the shop where
my favorite dress (it was calling my name) hung in the window. I told
Mother I did not want her and Daddy spending that kind of money on
my dress, but she insisted on returning to the store because she had an
idea. I should have known what it was!

She had me to try on the dress, took out her trusty small wire bound
notebook from her purse and began to sketch the garment's design. I
proudly wore the dress on my wedding day; it featured a fabulously long
scalloped lace train (two of my nephews, James and Eddy, served as

trainbearers) and every seed pearl was hand stitched. Mother even made the lace pillow, on which a third nephew, Donny, carried my ring.

Mother had a knack for a well-put-together look, a coordinated, simple classic look. It did not matter whether it was inexpensive costume jewelry or a suit made from a clearance rack; Susella Hickey Seals always looked like she stepped from the cover of a fashion magazine. She carried herself like a model. When she entered a room, every eye looked her way, but she was simply oblivious to the attention. I was never ashamed to introduce my mother to anyone.

One day, I remember, I swung by to pick up Mother to take her shopping. As I was about to drive off, Mother softly directed me to "put on a little lipstick." She told me whether I wore makeup or not, to wear lipstick and it would quickly give my appearance a lift. I've never forgotten her instructions, though I'm guilty of not always following them. There's something that tugs at my heart strings each time I apply lipstick; I smile and think of my exquisite looking mother.

A second example of Mother's simplicity in dress comes to mind when, during the last years of her life, many Sundays I assisted her in dressing for church. I was choosing jewelry and asked her about a bracelet.

"I feel better without one when wearing a long sleeved blouse with a ruffled cuff," she said. "I think the ruffle serves the same purpose as the bracelet."

And then she added sincerely, "You know I do not like to call attention to myself."

I've always thought it divinely ironic her lack of ostentation in fact had the opposite effect on people. What a wonderful role model she was!

Home

"She looketh well to the ways of her household
and eateth not the bread of idleness."
—Proverbs 31:27 (KJB)

"To be discreet, chaste, keepers at home, good obedient to their
own husbands, that the word of God be not blasphemed."
—Titus 2:5 (KJB)

"Distributing to the necessity of saints; given to hospitality."
—Romans 12:13 (KJB)

"Use hospitality one to another without grudging."
—I Peter 4:9 (KJB)

"Be not forgetful to entertain strangers; for thereby
some have entertained angels unawares."
—Hebrews 13:2 (KJB)

S USELLA LOVED HER HOME, AND being at home. She'd travel on
vacations, visit her sister in Florida, go with her husband to out-of-
town churches, but she most loved being at home. She repeatedly said
she didn't care how far away she traveled as long as she could be home
each night.

Mother enjoyed decorating her home. She had different looks
according to the season. Every Christmas always had a touch of
holiday in every room, and there was always some kind of snack or
treat available in case someone dropped in. There were spring/summer

window treatments as well as her fall/winter ones. But one thing was obvious. Home was filled with love and simple, genuine objects. She never decorated the house in an ostentatious way. Her home was filled with cherished items like gifts from family and friends. No matter how meager the item, Mother treated it as pure gold. This gracious woman wanted her home to be one where everyone felt comfortable.

Our home was also special because Mother practiced the gift of hospitality. Everyone, no matter their lot in life or reason for a visit, was welcomed with open arms. My father-in-law, now deceased, relished sharing the time he visited Mom and Dad's home, stating with great flourish that "Mrs. Seals put out a 'spread' like I'd never seen before." I recall on more than one occasion when our modest country church hosted regional association gatherings. Daddy, with a sincere pastor's heart, would announce before the benediction, "Now we don't want any of you, especially our out-of-towners, to go home before the next meeting. All of you just follow us home. We'll feed you and fellowship with you. In fact, we'll treat you in so many ways, you're bound to like one of them!" Mother would beam radiantly from her church pew. Many times it seemed as if the whole congregation took Daddy up on his offer, for I remember lots of people in our home.

When having overnight guests Mother made sure extra toiletries were laid out in case the visitor had forgotten an item. A ready snack and reading material were also placed in each room along with a nightlight or flashlight in case the occupant should have to get up in the middle of the night. Susella always rose early and prepared breakfast and offered coffee and juice for first risers. Like many other southern women, Mother made a breakfast delicacy called "chocolate gravy." It was customarily served piping hot with lots of butter and homemade biscuits. On these special mornings no one worried about calories when offered this regional favorite. All her grandchildren loved Mother's treat. On Facebook recently my emotions welled up within me while reading an exchange between two nephews about "Granny's Chocolate Gravy." One had sent the other her recipe for it.

In her later years Mother wrote down Bible verses, poems, or quotes from books or magazines and placed them conspicuously throughout her home. I asked her why she did this. She said the words encouraged her. I know they did me and others who might happen on them. About a year after Mother's passing I was having a particularly difficult day struggling with the grief of losing her. Crying and bearing my soul to God I expressed how much I missed her and wished I could hear her voice again. Suddenly I felt an urge to visit Daddy. I drove over to check on him, and he asked me to look for something in another room. To my amazement I discovered a box containing many years of Mamma's personal journals. I stayed up all night listening to Mother's voice in those pages and thanking God for His distinct answer to my prayer. Wings of comfort gently embraced me.

Here, in her handwriting, is Susella's recipe for chocolate gravy
which she called "Doodle Soup" for her grandchildren's enjoyment.
Grandson, Eddy, followed her directions and snapped a photo
of the finished product. It looks yummy don't you think?

Worship

I NEVER REMEMBER *NOT* GOING TO church. When you hear the word *worship* what first comes to mind? Each denomination has its own unique style of worship service. And no one denomination can claim the corner market on worship. My maternal grandfather, Papa Hickey, was an old fashioned Baptist preacher. I can remember when he would get "happy in the Lord" and laugh and shout and dance. It was magical to me because he conveyed such happiness. This is my first memory of someone worshiping God. My mother, on the other hand, was a quiet worshiper. I don't remember her ever shouting or dancing; she shed tears in quiet reverence.

My mother and her father represent, to me, the opposite ends of the worship spectrum. I know each was appropriate. As a result of these childhood experiences, I've come to appreciate various worship styles.

Each method is valid according to a person's personality and comfort level. We all know what speaks to us. Let's not judge another by their manner of religious devotion. We may not attend the same church for years as older generations once did. Sometimes God uses our faith walk to move us to another gathering of believers. I believe this is why God allows denominations. We are to find a body of Christ that most aligns with our means of reverencing God. Many times divisions occur within a congregation when worship practices observed are not congenial to the beliefs of even a small percentage of the assembly. In such situations I believe it is best to avoid promoting change that may cause a rift in the congregation, and seek out a house of worship where you feel closest to God, where you achieve the greatest peace. If God wishes to change a particular group of believers, He--through the Holy Spirit's working--will initiate the revision.

The point I wish to stress here is not the *method* of worship by which you feel close to God; rather, worship in a *way* that will inspire you to serve God and fellow human beings. This inspiration is the *authenticity* of worship. Wherever, whenever, and however you feel true emotion and love of God, this is your place of genuine worship, your home; and as the saying goes, "There's no place like home."

To sum up, presenting oneself as genuine can be achieved if the four areas discussed in the previous pages work in conjunction with one another.

Words: We should always realize the vital importance of our words.

Dress: Making a real fashion statement means "to thine own self be true." If you don't like a certain style, never let a salesperson convince you otherwise. Create a signature look through trial and error. When you admire the way someone dresses, tell them. It is a wonderful compliment to pay to someone.

Home: Integrity in your home is simply decorating to achieve daily comfort and ease for you and all who share the same roof. Genuine homes are not necessarily the ones filled with expensive furnishings. In a true home the atmosphere of love, peace, and laughter is the chief décor.

Worship: Genuine worship can be difficult if we attempt to practice it only in a house of worship. You also need to worship God in the privacy of your home.

The result: If you practice being yourself in talk, dress, home, and worship, peace and confidence will take up residence in your life.

REFLECTION EXERCISES:

1. Do you try to impress others by sometimes exaggerating facts?
2. During a lull in a conversation do you feel the need to fill up the empty air?
3. When a person asks for advice, do you accept that they may only want someone who will listen?
4. Are you willing to truly listen to another human being who needs to talk?
5. Is your appearance one you believe is pleasing to God?
6. Have you ever under or overstated what you paid for clothing or when wearing new clothing, claimed it was old when in fact you just allowed it to hang in the closet a really long time?
7. Do you make decisions in your home to impress others or to suit your family's needs?
8. Are you proud or ashamed to display a Bible in your home?
9. Does your definition of worship agree with God's word?
10. What steps can you take for daily worship?

CHAPTER 2

Love

"Beloved, let us love one another; for love is of God; and
every one that loveth is born of God and knoweth God."
—I John 4:7 (KJB)

THE DEFINITION OF *LOVE* IS a deep and ardent affection. Our
society so loosely flings this word around that it has become a
trite expression. I, however, have been most blessed in this key area.
I can honestly say there has never been a day I have not felt loved,
thanks to Mother and Daddy. No one else might care for me, but their
extravagant love has cushioned many hard blows.

Even as I work on final editing of this book, I am forced to rewrite
this portion because God just called Daddy home. God knew I wrote
this book as part of my grieving process with mother's loss in 2006 and
now, after almost giving up on seeing it in print, I received word it is
to be published. As the year winds down and we bury Daddy, maybe

God, in His omniscience knew putting final touches on this project would once again sooth my grief for the loss of my precious Daddy. He was ninety-two and the roles had reversed. I struggled with changes in our relationship just as I did with Mother. It's very hard to watch your parents who have lived vital and productive lives transform into creatures of frailty and dependency. There were innumerable days it was so gut wrenching I'd find myself physically ill. I adored Daddy as much as I did Mother. No matter my age, I was always "Daddy's little girl." Strangely there is a sentence I find I cannot delete as I type: *I still feel Daddy's love.* For many years, as an adult Sunday school teacher, I observed one particular area in which many people wrestle – the unconditional love of our Heavenly Father. I have concluded that each person's earthly father relationship bears a direct correlation with their God relationship. If we had a tyrant father, we think God stands at the ready to whip us into shape. If we've been fortunate to have a father who possessed genuine love, we can readily relate to a God who loves us no matter what. He has mercy, is willing to forgive, and is a Divine Papa (Abba in the Greek) of second, third, and many chances.

My parents' genuine affection for me has been the one constant in my life. Other areas of my life have traveled like a wild rollercoaster ride over the years. There once were years of perceived friends and loved ones. Other times I lived with ostracism by family, community, and church. Thank goodness Mother and Daddy rooted and grounded me in God's word. Their love and guidance taught me one important life principle: *Human beings will disappoint and hurt you, but God will neither leave you nor forsake you. God will always, always love you.*

There are four distinct spheres of life where Mother, as well as Daddy, illustrated deep and abiding love: *life, yourself, others, and forgiveness.*

Life

"The wise in heart shall be called prudent: and the
sweetness of the lips increaseth learning."
—Proverbs 16:21 (KJB)

"Death and life are in the power of the tongue: and
they that love it shall eat the fruit thereof.
—Proverbs 18:21 (KJB)

"And he shewed me a pure river of water of life, clear as
crystal, proceeding out of the throne of God and of the
Lamb. In the midst of the street of it, and on either side
of the river, was there the tree of life, which bare twelve
manners of fruits and yielded her fruit every month: and
the leaves of the tree were for the healing of the nations......
And whosoever will, let him take the water of life freely."
—Revelation 22:1, 2 and 17 (KJB)

"Who can understand his errors? Cleanse thou me from secret faults."
—Psalm 19:12 (KJB)

*"Three grand essentials to happiness in this life are something
to do, something to love and something to hope for."*
—Joseph Addison

W E ALL LOVE LIFE WHEN things are going well or as we had
planned. But what about those times when life sometimes
hands us lemons? Many of us tend to bite into the lemon and pucker

into a sourpuss face, forcing all around to sour also. But some, like Susella, made lemonade. To continue this analogy, let's look literally at how lemonade is made.

First of all, we must use a lemon, a bitter tasting fruit. We cannot make lemonade with any other fruit. You will get superb lemonade if you apply pressure to the lemon and roll it back and forth a few seconds to release the juices inside before slicing it. Second, sugar is added to the lemon. In cooking terms, it is best if you "muddle" the lemon and sugar by mashing the sugar and lemon together to meld the two flavors. This sweetness added to the bitter tasting fruit actually produces an unparalleled flavor. Finally, water is stirred into the mixture. If purified or sparkling water is used the result is one of the most refreshing and thirst quenching drinks ever swallowed on a sultry summer day.

What is the point I am trying to make? When life hands us lemons, roll the lemon (the problem, situation, person, etc.) around awhile, looking at all sides before slicing into it. Slice it; divide it into pros and cons. What exactly is the muddling part? Well, interestingly enough the word muddle means to confuse. If we are handed a difficult set of circumstances in life, sometimes we are confused because of bitterness, envy, and strife. You know what James 3:16 says? "For where envying and strife is, there is confusion and every evil work." (Lemons)

So what does the next ingredient, the sugar represent? Remember the old saying about catching more flies with honey than vinegar? The sweetness of Godly counsel can provide sweet nectar of help during life's woes. A divine word can come through any means God chooses, through reading His inspired word, through a trusted family member, friend, or pastor, even through nature or watching the words you personally speak. Mother reminded me regularly to be open to God's many ways of speaking to us.

Then there is the water, which could be indicative of new life, new beginnings, new wisdom to handle the situation, perhaps even a miracle. Remember Christ's first recorded miracle? At the marriage celebration in Cana, Jesus directed the stone pots to be filled with *water*.

And the water was turned to wine (John 2:1-11). Wine is a symbol of celebration even today. It represents making life fruitful or blessed. As Mother often reminded me, we never know how long we'll be here so we should enjoy life. It should be reveled for what it is – a gift of grace from God. Love it. Please love life!

Yourself

"For all the law is fulfilled in one word, even in this;
Thou shalt love thy neighbor as thyself?"
—Galatians 5:14 (KJB)

"Do not judge, or you too will be judged. For in the
same way you judge others, you will be judged, and with
the measure you use, it will be measured to you."
—Matthew 7: 1, 2 (NIV)

" You then, why do you judge your brother? Or
why do you look down on your brother? For we
will all stand before God's judgment seat."
—Romans 14:10 (NIV)

I F YOU HAVE EVER FLOWN, you recall the in flight safety instructions directed to all travelers with small children. We are told to put the oxygen mask on ourselves first, then place it on our children. This act is a perfect example of how we should be kind to ourselves.

So how do you love yourself? Please think about the question for a few seconds. If you think you've made too many mistakes and there is no help for you, you're wrong. As long as there is breath in your body, there is hope. All the people who love you, most importantly God, want you to know you are loveable. You are special. You have worth. You are here for a reason. Some people find their life path early on proceeding with seemingly clearly marked directions, while others discover a wrong turn here or a detour there; but if our personal GPS system is the Holy

Spirit, we eventually return to the proper course for our lives. Some, as Mother jokingly told my husband (because neither one had a good sense of direction), "We could get lost in an acre corn field." We need to make sure we have a good sense of direction either through discernment of the Holy Spirit, or godly counsel of some kind. Remember to think highly of yourself (not higher than others) and others will think highly of you too. If you happen to be trudging along and feel you have been falsely labeled a misfit, remember God and *you* know the truth. Believe you me, God and *you* make a majority. Truth will eventually prevail.

On the other hand, if you have taken that wrong turn, trust me when I say there is an answer for that too, even if you feel everyone thinks there is no hope. That very thing happened once to a woman in scripture. She was about to be stoned to death for being caught in the very act of wrongdoing. Everyone was ready to write her off and punish her accordingly. But Jesus came along and began writing on the ground. Many have speculated exactly what Jesus was writing. I've heard it might have been the Ten Commandments. One preacher theorized Jesus could have been writing down the wrongdoings of everyone ready to condemn her to death.

There is, however, another aspect of the story I would like to emphasize, though. If you read John 8 closely and look at verse six, it says, "as though he heard them not." Jesus paid no attention to the woman's accusers. But the accusers kept on until Jesus finally did speak to them: "He that is without sin among you, let him first cast a stone at her." Her accusers had to shamefully walk away. When Jesus asked the woman if she had anyone to condemn her, she said no, and Jesus told her neither did He, to go and sin no more.

When everyone else turns away from you, remember Jesus is still with you and this is reason to love yourself, hold your head up, and go on. Mother, as well as Daddy, helped me understand this principle through Biblical accounts and the scriptures.

Others

"A friend loveth at all times…."
—Proverbs 17:17 (KJB)

"A man that hath friends must shew himself friendly: and
there is a friend that sticketh closer than a brother."
—Proverbs 18:24 (KJB)

*"I have learned that to have a good friend is the purest of all
God's gifts, for it is a love that has no exchange of payment."*
—Frances Farmer

*"It is only through disruptions and confusion that we grow, jarred out of
ourselves by the collision of someone else's private world with our own."*
—Joyce Carol Oates

*"The proper office of a friend is to side with you when you are wrong.
Nearly anybody will side with you when you are in the right."*
—Mark Twain

LOVING OTHERS IS SOMETIMES A difficult task. Often others' attitudes and behaviors are so diametrically opposed to ours that we wonder how that person could ever be considered loveable. Mother taught me one great principle about others: *Everyone* just wants to be loved.

We have all encountered individuals who protest and say they don't care if anyone loves them. Mother believed that the loudest protesters are usually the ones who secretly most desire love. She would say that if their lives were just probed deeply enough, often we would discover hurtful incidences that occurred early in life, many times at the hands of the very ones they thought loved them. Mother assured me this pain could create a deep emotional scar often masked by seemingly reprehensible attitudes and behaviors. She drove home the importance of finding good in everyone. She explained that everyone has goodness in them; for some we just have to dig a little deeper to find it – but it is there. Always seek it out.

I must add that Daddy was known as a loving man. One of the most memorable sermons I ever heard him preach was on the love of God and loving one another that he delivered to our local church, after my parents moved closer to my husband and me so we could better care for them in their last years.

Here is the place I write honoring friendship. Immediately I begin by thinking of a quote from a perpetual calendar my dear friend, Barbara Hale, gifted me with several years ago. I do not know who to give credit for this saying, but it speaks to every fiber of my being regarding friendship:

> "A friend is there when everyone else isn't, believing when everyone else hasn't, understanding when everyone else doesn't, loving when everyone else wasn't."

The veracity to this statement, and the hands-on practice of it by my cherished friends, has provided me deep abiding solace during the most difficult periods of my life. It is true that one only discovers who their real friends are during bad times. A more recent time comes to mind when, after suffering a life changing fall while out of state, another precious sister friend, Shirley Green, was waiting in the driveway of our home. My husband pulled in after picking me up at the airport and had to physically carry me in the house because I was unable to walk. Shirley was there with food, words of encouragement, and everything we needed that first day home. God used her because my husband was definitely in 'overwhelm' mode after taking one look at me coming off the plane in a wheelchair. Shirley has been my friend since the age of five so we've weathered many things, good and bad.

Another friend I must mention is Kathy Hatfield. She and I will not talk for weeks, then the phone rings and it is a divine appointment. She has prayed many prayers for me because our friendship has also weathered the test of time and life's changes. One thing I know for sure is that this writer could never wish for better or more beautiful friends. It is one of my life's most wonderful mercies from God. I wish I could shower each of them with extravagant and unimaginable gifts. But since this is not feasible, during turns of prayer and meditation, I visualize each person while asking God to grant their goodly, yet possibly secret desires. I fully believe God can accomplish my requests. His blessings can be far superior to any present I could offer. My valued companions tenderly weave a beautiful tapestry of divine bliss into my existence.

Forgiveness

"For if you forgive men when they sin against you, your
heavenly Father will also forgive you. But if you do not forgive
men their sins, your Father will not forgive your sins."
—Matthew 6: 14, 15 (NIV)

"And be ye kind one to another, tenderhearted, forgiving one
another, even as God for Christ's sake hath forgiven you."
—Ephesians 4:32 (KJB)

"Let nothing be done through strife or vainglory; but in lowliness
of mind let each esteem others better than themselves."
—Philippians 2:3 (KJB)

"Forgiveness is the act of admitting we are like other people."
—Christina Baldwin

"The art of being wise is knowing what to overlook."
—William James

"Life only demands from you the strength you possess.
Only one feat is possible-not to have run away."
—Dag Hammarskjold

THE WORD *FORGIVE,* AS DEFINED in the dictionary, means to
stop feeling angry or resentful towards someone for an offense
or mistake. Personally, I offer this addendum: stop feeling angry or
resentful toward circumstances and events. All humankind identifies

with forgiveness to someone. This act is simply a matter of choice, not feelings. We either choose to forgive or not. I assert, equally, traumatic and precipitant events can deposit deep roots of bitterness into us. So, people *and* life occurrences must be saturated with surrender.

How can I make this summation? I have lived it! I believed with all my heart I had practiced the art of relinquishment of past offenses on the part of those hurting or angering me. But while compiling the subject matter of this section I realized there was still *something not quite right*. I searched for resolution through meditation, solitude, and scripture reading. Mother taught this routine to me and it really does work. I may have chosen to end my anger towards the people involved, but I still remained steeped in resentment of traumatic events that had swirled in and around my life in a short span of time. I believed it was just too much for any human to bear; and if one more person, even a stranger, told me to remember God doesn't put on us more than we can bear, I was convinced I would literally explode into a million pieces.

Suddenly in the quietness of pain, great clarity appeared. Once again, Mother's considerate character and loving wisdom flew from heaven to rest in my thoughts. She had taught me years earlier while going through a heart-breaking ordeal how to bear the unbearable. With tears in her eyes she told me that when it is simply too much, mentally wrap the burden up and picture placing it in Jesus' hands. If He bore *all* our sorrows on the cross, then does it not include *this one*? So I carefully wrapped this heartbreak in tears, inhaled a deep sigh of relief, and exhaled an even deeper sigh of release. I let it go! I gave it forward – I forgave! I share this lesson because possibly Satan has duped you also. He is the father of all liars, and perhaps he has you convinced you've dotted all i's and crossed your t's but still something is amiss. I urge you to give it forward, whatever it is: *forgive.*

This chapter moves in an eternal circle. First, repeat out loud the words, "God loves me, no matter what." By loving the sanctity of life and accepting God's love you can love yourself. If you struggle to love yourself, figure out the reason why. Scripture says love thy neighbor as thyself, so love yourself first so you can then love others. Once you begin to cherish yourself, do not be guilty of extremes. We've all dealt with those who have no problem loving themselves, but that is as far as it goes. We are expected to drop everything and cater to their every whim. This is not how we are to live according to God's word. The reason for loving forgiveness is that it cleanses the circular path to receive love from every direction. When we repent, ask forgiveness from God and accept Jesus, we are receiving God's supreme love gift. We are then freely able to love ourselves then love others (even our enemies), and the cycle continues.

REFLECTION EXERCISES:

1. Have you asked forgiveness from God and received Jesus Christ for eternity?
2. Do you love yourself? Why or why not?
3. How do you love your enemies?
4. Are there circumstances or someone you're unable to forgive?
5. Was the unforgiveable deed any worse than what you've done against God?
6. Will you sing "Jesus Loves Me" out loud?

CHAPTER 3

Joy

"Hitherto have ye asked nothing in my name: ask,
and ye shall receive, that your joy may be full."
—John 16:24 (KJB)

SUSELLA, MY MOTHER, RADIATED A joyous nature. One definition of *joy* is a condition of supreme well-being and good spirits. I never remember a time when Mother was not in a warm, genial mood. Yes, I saw her sad, heart-broken, or physically sick, but I am speaking in terms of her overall spirit. She did not complain. She could make me laugh; many times we both convulsed into giggles over the oddest things. Mama always seemed joyously peaceful no matter what. The following four key areas comprise particular truths this contented lady taught me about joy: *nature, work, play, solitude.*

Nature

"He hath made everything beautiful in his time: also he hath
set the world in their heart, so that no man can find out the
work that God maketh from the beginning to the end."
—Ecclesiastes 3:11 (KJB)

"Look at the birds of the air; they do not sow or reap or store away
in barns, and yet your heavenly Father feeds them. Are you no much
more valuable than they? Who of you by worrying can add a single
hour to his life? And why do you worry about clothes? See how the
lilies of the field grow. They do not labor or spin. Yet I tell you that
not even Solomon in all his splendor was dressed like one of these."
—Matthew 6:26-29 (NIV)

"The earth is the Lord's, and the fullness thereof;
the world, and they that dwell therein."
—Psalm 24:1 (KJB)

I HAVE ALWAYS BEEN A VORACIOUS reader, so it was never my first
inclination to appreciate nature. Mother surely sensed my lack of
interest early on and wanted to rectify the matter in her own sweet way.
She loved her flowers. She never asked for my help, but now looking
back I realize watching her care for them made me long for the feeling
that captured her rapturous gaze. Shortly after the Lord called Mama
home, to provide me solace I purchased rosebushes and tended them as
if they were the most important objects in the world. At that moment
in time, I'm convinced that they were.

Mother's signature flower was the pink rose. She had several varieties over the years, but for some reason she gravitated to the pink one and decorated a lot with it. Everyone had a knack for buying Mother pink-rose themed treasures. Even Susella's china was a pink rose pattern, which was passed on to my beautiful and Godly niece, Shelia.

Fresh flowers made Mother happy! She said so many times! I guess that's why they bring me such great joy, also. I figure if anything was good enough to make my mother happy, it is good enough for me too. Four distinct flowers say "Mother" to me. The first one is a rose, especially the pink one. When planting the memoriam rosebushes I chose a pink for her, yellow for my favorite, and red in honor of Daddy (red was his favorite color. I recall many gifts of red dresses from Daddy including some even after I was grown).The second flower that says "Mother" is the lilac. Each spring when I glimpse or smell lilacs, I go back in time when there was always a fresh lilac bouquet in the living room. The smell is intoxicating! The third flower is the iris. Long before studying Tennessee history Mother taught me that the iris is our state flower. I recall her explanations about different hybrids and how we snickered about the bearded iris.

The fourth flower that brings me great joy is one I learned about only during the last years of Mother's life. I tried my hand at raising dahlias, and to my delight I had great luck with them. Once, after taking a bouquet of dinner-plate-sized ones to her, Mother's eyes misted in tears. She believed I inherited my talent for growing these flowers from her mother, because each summer Grandma Pearl and her girlfriend tried to see who could grow the largest dahlia. My grandmother always grew the largest flower; Mother said she believed Grandma Pearl passed her talent on to me. That remembrance of my mother's words is a joyous filled moment I will always treasure.

*Here are the roses I planted a few weeks after Mother's
passing. Many days they've been watered with my tears.*

34 ⸙ SHARON S. TATE

Susella taught me about the Big Dipper, the Little Dipper and moon cycles on nights when the sky was drenched with glimmering stars. Mother once told me the twinkling stars were God winking at us and saying everything would be okay. That image always made me smile.

The spring before Mother's health took a turn for the worse, I have a wonderful 'nature memory.' We were in the midst of our regular morning phone confab. I was sitting outside, enjoying a beautiful spring morning, and rattling on to her. Mother suddenly asked, "Do you hear that?"

"What, Mother?" I asked, confused.

"Why, it's the redbirds saying, 'You're pretty, you're pretty.'"

The sweet woman's memorable words ring in my mind to this day each time I hear a redbird.

Work

"And that ye study to be quiet and to do your own business,
and to work with your own hands, as we commanded you."
—I Thess. 4:11 (KJB)

*"Far and away the best prize that life offers is the
chance to work hard at work worth doing."*
—*Theodore Roosevelt*

"Lives based on having are less free than lives based on doing or being."
—*William James*

*"Strive to be like a well-regulated watch: of pure gold,
with open face, busy hands, and full of good works."*
—*David C. Newquist*

Y OU MAY ASK HOW IT is ever possible to be full of joy at work. There's always the co-worker who seems to constantly sabotage your efforts, or the boss who overlooks and promotes the young one after you have given all the years of effort. Right? I'm sure you've probably thought at times about all the millions of dollars the sports and movie stars earn. Your mind said of course you would have joy if you made that kind of money. Well, please take a look back at the definition of joy above. It plainly says that joy is a condition of supreme well-being and good spirits. Not one mention of the word *money* is in the meaning of joy? To make my point, allow me to quote Elbert Hubbard: "We work to become, not to acquire."

Remember the universal question posed to every child:"What do you want to be when you grow up?" Think back on how you answered the question. Are you doing work that bears any resemblance to your childhood dreams? If you aren't, why not? The best advice I've ever heard is to find something you enjoy doing and figure out a way to get paid for it. We all have something we are passionate about, and if you are like me, the joy of doing it is payment enough. There is a fine line all must walk, however, when possessing special passions or talents. Never sell yourself short, or maybe I should say *free*. It's one thing to have a generous spirit, but beware of allowing people to take advantage of you. Your work does have value. But value for some of us is not necessarily monetary. My husband and I have been advocates of bartering for years. It is up to each of us, and obviously our present financial circumstances, to determine our value system.

The bottom line is this: in some way, somehow, find joy in your work. You may not like every aspect of your job, but look for those snatches of moments when time flies (and I do not mean the lunch break). Ask your supervisor if you can take on added responsibilities in those areas of your job you enjoy. If there is absolutely zero joy in every hour of every day in your present job, find a new job. My mother, however, always emphasized one thing about changing jobs: Find a new one while you still have one. It is one thing to be totally fed up and ready to walk away. It is another matter altogether to walk in and tell your family you've quit your job before landing a new one. This careless act only adds stress and strain to the family.

The economy is strained for so many right now. Many people have had no choice and were laid off. If you are in this situation, be open to try new things. You might just find a new passion and/or income. One final note about the hard economic times we are presently experiencing is that everyone who still has a job should be thankful and, yes, *joyous!* And if you apply the other basics discussed in this book--living in the present, having a grateful attitude, and living within our means--to your work environment, I promise that joy *will* enter your life.

Play

"A merry heart doeth good like a medicine......"
—Proverbs 17:22 (KJB)

"......a time to weep and a time to laugh...."
—Ecclesiastes 3:4 (KJB)

"No matter what your heartache may be, laughing
helps you forget it for a few seconds."
—*Red Skeleton*

"Joyfulness keeps the heart and face young. A good laugh makes
us better friends with ourselves and everybody around us."
—*Orison Swett Marden*

"There often seems to be a playfulness to wise people as if either
the equanimity has as its source this playfulness or the playfulness
flows from the equanimity; and they can persuade other people who
are in a state of agitation to calm down and manage a smile."
—*Edward Hoagland*

"We don't stop laughing because we grow old.
We grow old because we stop laughing.
—*Michael Pritchard*

"ALL WORK AND NO PLAY make Jack a dull boy." We've heard this axiom all our lives, but do we practice it? I've actually met people who boast about the quantity of unused vacation they've built up at work. I personally am not impressed. There is an inborn playful element in us all. We made use of it daily as children.

So what happened to it? Are we afraid the neighbors, the church or God will punish us if we take time to regroup, relax and have a sense of childlike play?

Remember, you're never too old to think about *not* acting your age. Stop stressing out! Yes, there are people who will attempt to take you for a ride in a guilt-mobile, but when they open the door and invite you in, pass on the trip. I want to share another Susella story to underscore my point. I spoke once with Mother about a situation at church. I told her how I felt that some brothers and sisters in the church were making me feel negligent about God because of my business responsibilities. This one particular gentleman told me how he let nothing keep him away from God's house. In seventeen years he had missed very few Sundays. Mother knew better than anyone how I loved to please and never wanted to disappoint my family, my church, and more importantly, my God. There was a very important business opportunity for me in an upcoming trip, not the least of which was a little vacation time thrown in for good measure. I told Mother how I was struggling with my decision. Mother began by asking me if I believed that Daddy was a good example of a man who was faithful to God. "Why, of course I do," I replied. Mother next said she wanted me to pray about my struggle, but remember how Daddy had handled travel time away from God's house. She guaranteed that God would provide me wisdom.

I followed her advice. As time drew closer to inform the powers that be at church, I told the gentleman I was not going to be there. I further informed him that I could never remember a time while growing up when I thought Daddy had put the parishioners ahead of his own family. I had great memories of family trips during some of his busiest years as a minister (at one point he pastored three churches in three different towns). I attended plenty of church services, but I never recall resenting them. I do recall laughing and having a good time on family vacations and on nearly every trip I was allowed to bring a friend along at Mother and Daddy's treat. These memories are precious to me as well as the tagalong friends who've shared their fond recollections of those vacation times.

In conversation with this beloved gentleman I learned there were grandchildren he had never seen because of his commitment to church. So I posed a question in kind reverence to this mighty servant of God: "When your children and grandchildren have to stand over you once God calls you home, do you think they will be proud of the fact you missed only five Sundays in seventeen years at church, or will they have fond memories of when Dad or Granddad visited, played, and experienced happy times with them?"

Please understand that I certainly was in no wise condemning him, for I love and respect this man very much. He may never admit it, but my question gave him pause for reflection. I am glad to report that less than a year later he traveled for two weeks to visit all his family in several states. He shared pictures with me when he returned; there were lots of happy smiling faces in the photographs!

What are your passions, interest, hobbies? Do you allot time for play? It seems we all lean to the serious side of life much too often. What makes you smile? Think about it for a moment. Do you enjoy music? Do you play a musical instrument? How long has it been since you picked it up? Put on music from your teen years and smile again. Create a feel good CD. Play it when you're down. There will be smiles instead of frowns. Watch a movie that tickles your funny bone. After all, remember God is the creator of that bone.

Solitude

"The wilderness and the solitary place shall be glad for them;
and the desert shall rejoice and blossom as the rose."
—Isaiah 35:1(KJB)

"But let it be the hidden man of the heart, in that which
is not corruptible, even the ornament of a meek and quiet
spirit, which is in the sight of God of great price."
—I Peter 3:4 (KJB)

"When he giveth quietness, who then can make trouble? And
when he hideth his face, who then can behold him? Whether
it be done against a nation, or against a man only"
—Job 34:29 (KJB)

Isn't it amazing the lengths many go to resisting to be alone? I can actually tell you I have heard individuals say they would rather be with a less than desirable person than be alone. Mother always asserted that I needed to know *me* before I tried to figure out my spouse. Boy, was she ever right!

Being alone will allow time to become acquainted with the real you, which can oft times be different from the person you present to the world. Make sure during your times of solitude that you establish your life goals. Ask God to bring you a mate with similar goals. You cannot and will not ever change a person after you marry them. Make sure you discuss everything that matters to you before the wedding. It will prevent future letdowns and heartbreaks. Trust me! Then there are those individuals who are happily content with the single life. If you have single friends like this, stop trying to fix them up. Allow them happiness right here and now.

Set aside a period of solitude each day. You will discover many amazing benefits. By clearing your mind of people and noise (televisions, telephones, computers, etc.) you will possess genuine clarity when decision making. Solutions will magically appear from previously cloudy thinking. Your discernment, extra-sensory perception, whatever you call it, will operate at an alarmingly accurate level. You will ask yourself, "Why hadn't I thought of this before?" I noticed Mother regularly practiced alone time right before retiring each evening. This bit of time helped her give any worries she had during the day to God, to clear her mind for sleep. Other people practice solitude first thing in the morning. Experiment and find out what works best for you.

I encourage you to try alone time for a thirty day experiment. Start off with five-minute segments, especially for those of you who regularly and frantically fill the air with noise and activity. You will neither lose your mind nor be struck by lightning. Make sure you are in a spot peaceful to you. It can be outdoors or in. As a matter of fact, I have several areas around my home where I practice the art of enjoying my own company, inviting my Heavenly Father along. I start often with praise and thankfulness to God in worship. Many times I remain in this state. Other times I proceed with intercessory prayers. Sometimes I read and meditate on scriptures. If I'm in a favorite outdoor area, I listen to God in nature and drink in the beauty of my surroundings. Continuing the experiment you can increase your time of solitude as you feel more comfortable. I promise it is a soothing liberating custom. It could potentially change your life! Try it for me in honor of my mother.

God's lessons for joy abound everywhere in nature. Learn from them. Watch ants, birds, squirrels, and all His creatures. Incorporate these lessons into your work, play, and times of solitude. For example, animals begin early. They stop and play along the way. Notice that birds generally sing on a lone tree branch. Their singing in solitude is joy in action. It doesn't sound like the blues to me. It's more like "I've got that joy, joy, joy, joy down in my heart, down in my heart to stay." The joy of the Lord is our strength.

Reflection Exercises:

1. Will you go outdoors and observe nature for ten minutes? Take your camera.
2. List three work responsibilities you enjoy. How can you assume more duties in these areas?
3. What did you enjoy doing playfully as a child? How can you incorporate that play into your adult life?
4. Are you uncomfortable being by yourself? For the next month practice alone time, starting with five-minute increments, then slowly increasing your solitude each successive week.

Chapter 4

Peace

"Thou wilt keep him in perfect peace, whose mind is
stayed on thee: because he trusteth in thee."
—Isaiah 26:3 (KJB)

*P*EACE IS FREEDOM FROM DISTURBANCE. *Peace* is everyone's hope for our planet. But before we can expect tranquility for the world, serenity must first reside within us. I can tell you my childhood was one of great peace. Any uneasiness on my part was self-imposed, nothing resulting from life with Daddy and Mother. All who came in contact with Mom said she was one of the most peaceful humans they had ever met. I agree and want to share the groundwork upon which my parents built a peaceful life. These building blocks provide a solid foundation upon which to build other vital life strata. If these four families of peace can be attained, the rest is easily reached for an existence of peace even in the midst of life's storms. It will be like the children's story, "The Three Little Pigs." Striving for peace with these bricks, all the huffing and puffing of life's winds will be unable to blow down our house of peace.

The Past

"Brethren, I count not myself to have apprehended: but this one thing I do, forgetting those things which are behind, and reaching forth unto those things which are before,"
—Philippians 3:13 (KJB)

"The definition of insanity is doing the same thing over and over and over and over again, but expecting a different result."
—Albert Einstein

"Good judgment comes from experience. Experience comes from bad judgment."
—Jim Horning

"There will come a time when you believe everything is finished. That will be the beginning."
—Louis L'Amour

ALL OF US HAVE REGRETS. Mistakes have been made. Decisions wrought have been wrong. Words have stung others with pain. Circumstances have come up that are completely out of our control. Maybe you and I are alike. This is an area of difficulty. I have always wanted to take care of things for others and myself. I guess I have that much of Mother and Daddy in me. But when those times dawn which are utterly out of our hands, they test our powers of endurance and most assuredly our peace of mind. Rehashing everything we've done wrong in the past will in no way change the outcome.

Why we do this I'm not really sure. Maybe we believe if we

continuously go over and over the past, what went wrong will materialize. We want to decide definitely we were right, the other person was wrong, and then we'll feel better. Possibly we try to identify the exact moment things went awry so the error won't be repeated. For whatever reason, I encourage you to stop. The past is exactly that – past. All the mental kicking ourselves only keeps us stuck in rewind. And long as the rewind button is functioning, we cannot punch the play button for peace now. If you know you were wrong, admit it. This is healing. Apologize to yourself, just like you would to someone else. Forgive yourself! If you need to make amends with someone else regarding something in the past, do so right away. It is easier the quicker you do it. Learn the lesson, file it in your life history, and move on. With permission, I give you an excerpt from Eckhart Tolle's book, *The Power of Now:*

"Does the past take up a great deal of your attention? Do you frequently talk and think about it, either positively or negatively...... Then you are not only reinforcing a false sense of self but also helping to accelerate your body's aging process by creating an accumulation of past in your psyche."

The Present

"For he saith, I have heard thee in a time accepted, and in the day of salvation have I succored thee: behold, now is the accepted time: behold, *now* (italics mine) is the day of salvation."
—II Corinthians 6:2 (KJB)

"How simple it is to see that all the worry in the world cannot control the future. How simple it is to see that we can only be happy now, and that there will never be a time when it is not now."
—*Gerald Jampolsky*

I N ORDER TO PARTICIPATE IN peace with the present, please reread the previous section. Be confident you have dealt with any unfinished business of the past. Otherwise you will be like many who only speak in terms of used to be. This act of dealing with the past is crucial. Deal with it in a manner that speaks and helps you once and for all know the past is *a slice* of your life, not the *whole* enchilada.

The best way I can encourage you to have peace with the present is to remember an old saying we've all heard: "Forget about the past, don't worry about the future, cherish the present. That's why it is called the *present*. It is a gift." The present is all we know for sure we have--right now. So many of us are still either living in the past or worrying about the future and we forget to enjoy presence of the present. Again I quote Eckhart Tolle's *The Power of Now:*

"As soon as you honor the present moment, all unhappiness and struggle dissolve, and life begins to flow with joy and ease. When you act out of present-moment awareness, whatever you do becomes imbued with a sense of quality, care and love – even the most simple action."

Mother generated a peaceful look no matter the task at hand. After reading Mr. Tolle's book I now better understand why.

The Future

"Boast not thyself of tomorrow; for thou knowest
not what a day may bring forth."
—Proverbs 27:1 (KJB)

"Therefore do not worry about tomorrow for tomorrow will
worry about itself. Each day has enough trouble of its own."
—Matthew 6:34 (NIV)

"Whereas ye know not what shall be on the morrow.
For what is your life? It is even a vapour, that appeareth
for a little time, and then vanisheth away."
—James 4:14 (KJB)

*"Here is the test to find whether your mission on
earth is finished: if you're alive, it isn't."*
—Richard Bach

TO INITIATE THE PROCESS OF peace with our future please refer to the above scriptures. There is no peril in generating goals to accomplish down the road. Doing so provides direction and focus in our lives. Road blocks appear suddenly when we spend so much time living for the future we never enjoy here and now. After all, here and now is all we have. Mother regularly reminded me of this fact. No wonder so many of us are depressed because tomorrow never comes. I reiterate: concern for tomorrow is stealing joy and peace from today. Again Eckhart Tolle tells us that "stress is caused by being 'here' but wanting to be 'there,' or being in the present but wanting to be in the future." This desire fashions a divide in our mind, and Jesus said in Matthew 12:25, "Every kingdom divided against itself is brought to desolation; and every city or house divided against itself shall not stand." We all want to stand strong, so remember creating a division in our mind worrying over the future results in lack of confidence and the appearance of "you look like you've got the weight of the world on your shoulders." Please remember only One is the True Proprietor of such a weight. You can remember Who by simply singing anew the childhood song "He's got the whole world in His hands."

Here are the lyrics to one of my favorite old hymns "I Know Who Holds Tomorrow" (words and music by Ira Stanphill):

"I don't know about tomorrow, I just live from day to day;
I don't borrow from its sunshine, for its skies may turn to gray;
I don't worry o'er the future, for I know what Jesus said;
And today I'll walk beside Him, for He knows what is ahead.
I don't know about tomorrow, it may bring me poverty;
But the one who feeds the sparrow, is the one who stands by me;
And the path that be my portion, may be through the flame or flood;
But His presence goes before me, and I'm covered with His blood.

Chorus:

Many things about tomorrow, I don't seem to understand;
But I know who holds tomorrow, and I know who holds my hand."

Uncertainty

"Finally brethren, whatsoever things are true, whatsoever
things are honest, whatsoever things are just, whatsoever
things are pure; whatsoever things are lovely, whatsoever
things are of good report; if there be any virtue, and
if there be any praise, think on these things."
—Philippians 4:8 (KJB)

"Peace I leave with you; my peace I give you. I do
not give to you as the world gives. Do not let your
hearts be troubled and do not be afraid."
—John 14:27 (NIV)

"Being confident (certain) of this very thing, that
he which hath begun a good work in you will
perform it until the day of Jesus Christ."
—Phil. 1:6 (KJB)

*"It may be that when we no longer know what to do, we
have come to our real work: and when we no longer know
which way to go, we have begun our real journey."*
—*Wendell Berry*

Y OU MAY THINK THIS HEADING should be a part of peace with the
future. Future's uncertainty often creates a sense of instability.
Paradoxically the past can spur hesitancy too. It is more than mere
positive thinking, though we should know our actions are servants to
our thinking. Dubiousness can cause us great angst. Doubt can rule

our every move. It may be a mindset held from generational thinking. Our parents, our parents' parents, and our great grandparents may have lived, moved, and had their beings in this logic. Now is the time to break the generational curse. Just because we've always done it this way is no longer an excuse. It could have resulted from duplicitous incidents in our lives. We don't trust anyone anymore. We can go back thirty years and cite wrong after wrong, happening after happening. Is this how you want to be remembered, how you wear the whiners hat with distinction? Now is the time to recant and choose forgiveness. This is the moment to change your mind. We are allowed to change our way of thinking, right?

So what should we think about? Read Philippians 4:8 again.

Allow me to simplify my message. If we think on the opposite of each of these words we will infinitely live in uncertainty: lies instead of truth, dishonesty for honesty, injustice opposed to justness, impurity versus purity, no loveliness alternately for lovely, bad reports in place of good reports. When recidivism creeps in, we must stop, ask ourselves which one of the antonyms has taken residence, and kindly request its departure by dwelling on the higher train of thought in Jesus' name. Peace will then ensue.

Peace is the desire of everyone. Jesus Christ is the Prince of Peace; Satan is the prince of every opposite feeling of peace. We can't always trust our feelings. As humans we are made up of a body, soul, and spirit. Our feelings are a part of our mind, will, and emotions and they can be subverted by the wiles of the devil. Mother often said one thing is certain – uncertainty. If you have received salvation you can experience peace with all things because Jesus died once for all past, present, and future. Uncertainty is then transformed into confidence in the Redeemer.

REFLECTION EXERCISES:

1. What are you still struggling with in your past? Have you prayed? If not, ask for peace, forgiveness, deliverance, etc. Be specific with the need.

2. What is presently hindering your peace? Give it to God.
3. Name what most concerns you about your future.
4. What steps can you take to alleviate it?
5. Name the one uncertainty thwarting your peace.
6. Can you counsel and pray with a Godly friend or pastor?

CHAPTER 5

Listen To God

"And thine ears shall hear a word behind thee saying,
This is the way, walk ye in it, when ye turn to the
right hand, and when ye turn to the left."
—Isaiah 30:21 (KJB)

"The righteous shall flourish like the palm tree….."
—Psalm 92:12 (KJB)

EVER MORE SO THAN NOW, we live in a convoluted society. When books are written by the thousands, secular publishers hesitate to print books even hinting at a divine and Almighty Power named God. If you notice, even some of today's best sellers have watered down their theological beliefs, calling God by more politically correct names, and many times without realizing it, the authors use new age terminology in order to appeal to the masses, not offend anyone, and coddle their publishers. I do not propound in this book to offend anyone. I feel just as Mother did when quoted in a church newsletter featuring Mother and Daddy's life: "I just couldn't stand it if I thought I had hurt someone's feelings." I want everyone to be in peace. However, as a born again Christian I offer the following scripture to personally go on record of whom I acknowledge as God:

> "I, therefore, the prisoner of the Lord, beseech you that we walk worthy of the vocation wherewith ye are called, with all lowliness and meekness, with longsuffering, forbearing one another in love; Endeavoring to keep the unity of the Spirit in the bond of peace. There is one body, and one Spirit, even as ye are called in one hope of your calling; One Lord, one faith, one baptism, One God and Father of all, who is above all, and through all, and in you all." Ephesians 4: 1-6 (KJB)

This is who I follow. This is who Mother and Daddy taught me is God. I do not apologize for it. In fact, I would be dead and you would not be reading these words had I not had a close encounter with the one True God. Mother instructed me when I was real little to listen for God's voice. I asked her when I needed to be quiet. Rather than repeat what my sister, Linda, and my brother, Harold, would have said--"all the time"--Mother suggested that each night during my prayers to listen for God. After many nights of listening, tilting my head on my pillow, straining to hear the slightest sound, I had handled all I could stand and started crying. Mother came to my bedside, cradled me in her arms, and asked what was wrong. I dejectedly sobbed that God doesn't tell me anything. "I listen real hard every night and I can't hear one word."

Mom chuckled and told me in her soothing voice, "He drops thoughts into your little mind. When you read your Bible you are listening to God, and sometimes God uses other folks to say things to us. Okay? Mother is sorry. I didn't make myself very clear, did I?"

She never said anything like I had misunderstood her or I wasn't listening. During my childhood I never remember a single time I felt belittled, only encouraged.

Consequently, I understood far earlier in life than many how to hear from God. And equally important, at a very young age, I understood the concept that God listens to us. I can't remember exactly how old I was because our family never speaks much of this time, but I remember Daddy sitting me down while Mother was out. My sister and brother were already grown and out of the house, so I was the last child left at home. Daddy explained to me that Mother had a health problem. (One of Mother's brothers had been sent home from Germany in World War II with tuberculosis to die.) Mother had tested positive for TB more than once. The next course of action according to protocol during the late 1950s was a tuberculosis sanitarium. Daddy explained that the doctors were saying this was to follow for Mother. I began crying. Daddy sat me on his lap, stroked my hair, and said, "Now, Sherry, you believe in God, don't you?"

"Yes, Daddy" I replied.

"Then you and I are going to kneel down right now by this couch and we're going to pray to God asking him not only to keep Mother here at home with us but to heal her body and rid it of this TB. All right?"

When I asked Daddy how I should say it, he told me to ask God just like I was asking him for something. I went first, crying, telling God how much I loved my Mama. I explained I couldn't handle life without Mother with me every day. Daddy and the rest of my family needed her too. I remember telling God I didn't care how He did it, but to convince those doctors Mother had to stay home with us.

The following week as the doctors tested Mother one final time, do you know what happened? The test was negative and Mother never mentioned it again. This was powerful stuff to a young impressionable mind. I'm not going to say I have listened explicitly every time I believe God has spoken to me because God knows I have made many mistakes in my life. I have lived long enough and had enough surreal experiences to know God can speak through any means He chooses.

Another powerful example of this is a recap of an experience I walked through many years ago. My husband was allowing someone to invade our marriage and my heart was breaking. I had begged and pleaded with God to deal with my husband and cause him to straighten up and fly right. During this time Mother and Daddy traveled with my husband and I to Florida. Once we had arrived at the beach (one of my favorite places on earth where I feel so close to God), Mother and I went walking. I was sharing with her how I had overheard my husband talking with this person on the phone. Mother, in her sweet gentle way, told me I had to truly turn it over to God. When I asked her how to know when I had honestly accomplished this, she painted this picture for me. "Well, it's like if you and I lived in different towns. You need one hundred dollars and write me asking for the money. You address, stamp, and mail the letter. An hour later you run back to the mailbox and rummage around until you retrieve it. Day after day you talk about writing Mother. You tell everyone you've asked Mother for one hundred dollars, but you wonder when she is going to send it. Actually, you never mailed the letter. You just talked about it. Once you mail it, expect an answer."

Later that night after my parents went to bed, I told my husband I was going for a walk on the beach. We agreed on a time when I was to be back. It was peaceful, but the sound of the surf drowned out my audible sobs to God.

"God please speak to me!" I wailed.

Then in my mind, as Mother had taught me so many years ago, a questioning thought broke through: "Do you see that patch of three palm trees in front of you? Look closely and meditate. Be mindful of how these three palm trees represent your husband, you, and this third person and the way you see the situation currently."

"Okay," I thought, "You're right. The tallest palm represents my husband, next tallest leaning towards it represents me as I am leaning toward my husband; and the third tree represents the person coming between James and me, since this tree seemed to be leaning directly in between the two taller palms."

The thought popped into my mind to walk around with the ocean to my back and face these same three palms, viewing them from a different perspective. As I stood with my back to the sea, the hairs on my arms stood up as I realized from this view the third palm that seemed to be coming between the taller trees was not actually coming between them at all; it was actually leaning *away* from the two tall ones! It was not even growing on the same clump of sea grass where the other two were standing. At this point I caught myself asking out loud, "God is this really You speaking to me, or am I just conjuring this up to help me through this?"

Then just as sure as if a human being had walked up to me and spoken I heard, "I know you're smart, but you're not *that* smart."

I jumped and whirled around laughing aloud, realizing that if there actually was a human being anywhere close they would think someone is home but the lights are not on. But no one was there, just God and me.

"Now go back to your husband," He said. "Rest well. In the morning before you say a word to anyone go out on your balcony and look at these three palm trees from my vantage point."

When I walked into our bedroom later, my husband quizzically asked if I was all right. "Yes," I answered. "Why do you ask?"

"You have the strangest look on your face," he responded.

"We'll talk about it tomorrow," I promised as I climbed into bed and slept the best I had in months.

The next morning was just as powerful. The minute my feet hit the floor I rushed outside to the balcony to view my precious palm trio. What a glorious sight! From the balcony tree number three not only was not a part of the other two, it seemingly was leaning backwards away from them. It didn't look quite as strong as it had from the other views. I never questioned God about this situation ever again. Not only did God resolve the issue, He provided an even more profound epilogue to this story. Approximately four or five years later, while traveling to the same Florida town with Judy Bunch, my soul sister (a sister who is not biological but should have been), we both rushed out to the balcony with the childish excitement we always exhibit when first arriving at the beach. While scanning the horizon I realized to my astonishment we were staying only steps away from my 'God speaking through the palm trees' moment, which, of course, I had shared with her. We both said at the same time, "Let's go see if the clump of palms is still here."

To get a better handle on the exact location of the divine palms I visually located the resort from the previous visit. Once again I had chills cover my body. "Judy, oh look!" I squealed with excitement, for the third palm tree had fallen and died, representing the death of Satan's attempts to destroy our marriage. Judy immediately snapped a picture so we could forever have proof that God speaks not only through burning bushes but also palm trees.

We have to be ready, willing and able to hear Him through whatever means He so chooses.

Wise Advice

"Bear ye one another's burdens and so fulfill the law of Christ."
—Galatians 6:2 (KJB)

"Praise be to the God and father of our Lord Jesus Christ, the Father of compassion and the God of all comfort, who comforts us in all our troubles, so that we can comfort those in any trouble with the comfort we ourselves have received from God."
—2 Corinthians 1:3,4 (KJB)"

"Each friend represents a world in us, a world possibly not born until they arrive, and it is only by this meeting that a new world is born."
—Anais Nin

H AVE YOU EVER HAD AN acquaintance say, "Tell me what to do"? It puts pressure on you, doesn't it? Mother taught me early to never tell someone else what to do. She told me, in the end we have to live with our own decisions. If we depend on someone else and it is wrong advice, probably two things will happen. One, we'll always blame that person for telling us wrong, and, two, it will many times put a wedge in the relationship or even end it.

There is nothing wrong with discussing all choices available. Often when in throes of decision making all possible options may not present themselves with clarity. If it is a traumatic event demanding a decision we can be in a brain fog. Equally mystifying is when good happens with choices to be made, we are so elated and caught up in the blessing we may not be thinking clearly. Why else do you think people who have received huge lottery winnings end up penniless years later?

Wise counsel is important. But how do we know who can provide wise counsel? The most important piece of advice Mother ever gave me in this area is to seek out someone who has journeyed down the same road you've traveled, but not just anyone who has lived your similitude. She schooled me to find someone I believed had handled a similar experience in a mature and wise manner. It is not always easy to discover this vis-à-vis because if it was a trying or particularly embarrassing ordeal, not just anyone wants the world to know what they have been through. But if you ask God to send you someone who can understand your situation, you will be astounded how many times He can provide answers at indiscriminate times from the least expected sources.

I have discovered that many people will gladly talk about even the worst circumstances if they believe you are genuinely seeking help. I must point out this is not the time to go into all the details of your trial. Mother's instructions were to really listen to the other person's story. It may be the first time the person has ever been asked to tell it. Even if it is a difficult story there are lessons to be learned, and most people feel better getting it off their chest. It could be an account this person has been forced to keep inside for years. Be the burden bearer in the midst of your own determinations. You might make a lifetime friend. There is nothing more powerful than the club of equivalency, a kindred spirit. This is why support groups are such a success. Only someone who has walked a similar path can provide true empathy in your situation. Listening in this manner can prove to be a powerful tool in your life walk.

Circumstances

"And we know that all things work together for good to them that
love God, to them who are the called according to his purpose."
—Romans 8:28 (NIV)

"For God hath not given us the spirit of fear; but of
power, and of love, and of a sound mind."
—II Timothy 1:7 (KJB)

"Casting down imaginations, and every high thing that
exalteth itself against the knowledge of God, and bringing
into captivity every thought to the obedience of Christ."
—II Corinthians 10:5 (KJB)

"Be strong and of a good courage, fear not, nor be afraid
of them: for the Lord thy God, he it is that doth go
with thee; he will not fail thee, nor forsake thee."
—Deut. 31: 6 (KJB)

A S PREVIOUSLY RELATED, IT IS amazing how some of life's
circumstances can dramatically change the course of our lives.
We seemingly have a handle on our life view. Then one day certain
happenings abruptly cause us to question every single article in our
personal belief system. Events can cause everyone and everything
to suddenly become so foreign to us that our minds begin to play
tricks on us. We are filled with fear and confusion. Depending on
the circumstances doubt, distrust, and even bitterness creep into our
thinking. This is a deep dark hole, and if we remain here neither good

nor lessons meant to be learned will take place. If this stagnant mind set continues a breakdown physically or mentally (or both) can be the result. So pay close attention to life events. Deal with them through any medium God so chooses to speak, but continue hearing with keen perception accompanied by thoughts of hope. This trial has not appeared for naught; there is a purpose. Seek the truth and remain courageous in the matter. Mother always told me I had courage, so I always tried to measure up to her assessment. In case no one has ever said it to you, you have courage. Courage is like faith. God's word tells us He has dealt to every man the measure of faith (Romans 12:3). I'm convinced He has also given each of us a measure of courage. We must choose to use it. You do possess moxie! I know you do; and deep down, you know it too!

One's Heart

"Thou hast proved mine heart; thou hast visited me in
the night; thou hast tried me, and shalt find nothing, I
am purposed that my mouth shall not transgress."
—Psalm 17:3 (KJB)

"Trust in the Lord with all thine heart: and lean
not unto thine own understanding."
—Proverbs 3:5 (KJB)

"And ye shall seek me, and find me, when ye
shall search for me with all your heart."
—Jeremiah 29:13 (KJB)

"Howbeit when he, the Spirit of truth is come, he will guide you into
all truth: for he shall not speak of himself; but whatsoever he shall
hear, that shall he speak: and he will shew you things to come."
—John 16:13 (KJB)

"And hereby we know that we are of the truth,
and shall assure our hearts before him."
—I John 3:19 (KJB)

"The ear that heareth the reproof of life abideth among the wise."
—Proverbs 15:31(KJB)

W E HAVE ALL HEARD THE adage "listen to your heart." But what
does it exactly mean? *The Vines Expository* says the word *heart*

came to represent man's entire mental and moral compass, both rational and emotional. In the Bible it is a picture of our personal inward life, "the hidden man or woman" including human depravity where sin resides. But mysteriously Scripture also "regards the heart as the sphere of Divine influence (Romans 2:15) and includes emotions, reasoning, and the will." To me, the heart is our all-encompassing compass. If we are rooted and grounded in God's word our compass will function properly and provide accurate directions when we seek them.

Once I asked Mother what she meant when she said listen to your heart. Her reply was simple. "Listen to what's right. It does not promote sin of any kind. It promotes peace. We all if possessing half a brain know this is truth at the most basic level. Remember the age old management acronym KISS (keep it simple stupid)?" Mother and I had another acronym *Keep it Simple Sharon.* I offer you one more – *Keep It Simple Saint.*

We must all be vigilant about guarding our heart. Keep the garbage out. Garbage in, garbage out, isn't this right? If we watch what we read, listen to, whom we associate with, and guard our principles we can be convinced when the time comes: listen to our heart. It will prove trustworthy.

When we put a premium on commitment to listening to God by regularly studying His word there will be no confusion. God is not the author of confusion. We can know His will. As a result, when listening to wise advice, looking at circumstances, and listening to our heart we can have the mind of Christ. Then when the enemy tries to trip us up, the Holy Spirit, as our teacher, will bring to mind a scripture giving us wisdom. We can discern if what we hear is truth.

REFLECTION EXERCISES:

1. Name a time you believe you heard directly from God. How did God speak to you? Do you continue to seek the same manner or are you open to new ways to hear from God?
2. Looking back name one you now know gave you wise advice.

Have you ever thanked them? If not, do so now with a call, letter, or gift.

3. What circumstances are presently speaking to you? What do you think God is trying to teach you?

4. What is speaking loudest to your heart right now? How can you honor this? What thoughts, words or deeds can you give to God?

CHAPTER 6

Acceptance

"To the praise of the glory of his grace, wherein
he hath made us accepted in the beloved."
—Ephesians 1:6 (KJB)

*A*CCEPTANCE REPRESENTS THE ACT OF taking or receiving something; favorable reception or approval; the act of believing. Four areas of life present opportunities for practicing the art of acceptance: *humankind, changes, compliments, rejection.* They can be challenging. Mother proved to be a good taskmaster for my learning. Allow me to share what I mean.

Humankind

"That there should be no schism in the body; but that the
members should have the same care one for another."
—I Corinthians 12:25-26 (KJB)

"Be of the same mind one toward another. Mind not high things, but
condescend to men of low estate. Be not wise in your own conceits."
—Romans 12:16 (KJB)

"Let nothing be done through strife or vainglory; but in lowliness
of mind let each esteem others better than themselves."
—Philippians 2:3 (KJB)

"Then Peter began to speak: "I now realize how true it is
that God does not show favoritism but accepts men from
every nation who fear him and do what is right."
—Acts 10:34, 35 (NIV)

"For there is no difference between Jew and Gentile – the same
Lord is Lord of all and richly blesses all who call on him."
—Romans 10:12 (NIV)

MOTHER AND DADDY TOLD ME many times growing up never to
think myself better than anyone, but always remember that I
was as good as anyone. I understand and appreciate the message they
were trying to communicate. I've thought a lot about the statement and
realize it is a wonderfully all inclusive notion. It is right up there with
"the playing field is level at the foot of the cross." Wouldn't the world

be more peaceful if this idea was adopted? I realize that my parent's one statement to me helped throughout many trying and peculiar circumstances in my life.

One particular incident comes to mind. I was in my late twenties, divorced, trying to make a life for myself. Taking a new corporate job, I was assigned an assistant who just happened to be African-American. She was a delightful young lady. We hit it off instantly. I had been experiencing health problems and was unable to be at the office, so she came to my apartment where I was recuperating. We had just finished a day's work. I asked her if she might be able to drive me back to my hometown so I could complete my recovery at Mother and Daddy's (I always seemed to feel better there.) She had the most pain stricken look on her face. I apologized for seemingly overstepping the lines, but her reassuring reply was steeped with emotion. She replied she would love to meet my Mother and Daddy because any couple who had raised a daughter in an all-white town with my sense of acceptance had to be a real special couple. In that one simple moment I realized what a unique and precious gift I possessed in my parents. Steeped in the South, where lots of racial prejudices existed, I was blessed indeed with Christian examples of acceptance. I knew they understood God's love.

I shared the story with Mother the next time we talked. She expressed her pride in my seeing the beauty of this girl and accepting her in my life with no strings attached. I give all credit to Mother and Daddy for teaching me to accept people who are not all just like me. Mother would remind me often that most people are doing the best they can under their circumstances. We have no idea what someone is going through. Just be real good to everyone. We all have bad and good days. So accept people, warts and all. I hope you accept me as you read this book.

Changes

"For our light affliction, which is but for a moment, worketh
for us a far more exceeding and eternal weight of glory." '
—II Corinthians 4:17 (KJB)

"That ye may be the children of your Father which is in
heaven for He maketh his sun to rise on the evil and on the
good and sendeth rain on the just and on the unjust."
—Matthew 5:45 (KJB)

"Facing it, always facing it, that's the way to get through. Face it."
—Joseph Conrad

*"Life isn't about waiting for the storms to pass, it's
about learning to dance in the rain."*
—Unknown

I T IS A RED LETTER day when good changes come our way. Everyone
likes a winner. When good things occur it is only natural to claim an
alliance to those to whom the good has happened. But sometimes even
good times offer their set of obstacles to overcome. We must deal with
that ever present green eyed monster, jealousy. This monster can rear its
head at the most inadvertent moments, coming often out of nowhere.
It sometimes rises in us. We should learn to identify the signs of our
own idiosyncrasies for dealing with it head-on so we can better handle
it should we be on the receiving end at some point.

We must accept good things in life with a great deal of aplomb.
By doing so during blessed times we are making major deposits into

our well of hope for making withdrawals during unpleasant periods. Trust me, there will be trying changes in all our lives. If you've neither experienced a time of despair nor are presently going through one, as sure as night follows day you will some day in the future. Those challenging shifts are different matters to different people. It is all a matter of perspective. What is gut-wrenching to one person might only be a blip on life's radar for another. Consequently none of us should invalidate a person's genuine emotions assailing them at such a crucial time. Whether we agree or disagree with the individuals' reactions should be irrelevant unless there is cause of bodily harm to themselves or others. We should simply stand sentinel and be available in whatever capacity of need arising, no matter how seemingly trivial or mundane. How many times have you heard "it's only puppy love"? Remember: it's important to the puppy. God's word says judge not that ye be not judged.

A second important factor is timing. We all have faced certain life events when we believed they were the worst possible scenario only to discover maybe years later the events were not nearly as burdensome as we originally thought. A final vital element regarding life changes is to remember we are not all at the same level of maturity or experience. Mother's difficult health issues are a classic example of my conviction. I've never handled myself well while being ill (Who does?). I tend to feel sorry for myself. I asked Mother how she was able to never complain when she felt bad. Her response was simply that she had had lots of opportunities to practice. I pondered her statement for weeks. It both convicted and awed me. Let's hope we build on our experiences, growing stronger with each year and every change, be it good or, as Mother put it, opportunistic.

Compliments

"A man hath joy by the answer of his mouth; and a
word spoken in due season, how good is it!"
—Proverbs 15:23 (KJB)

HAVE YOU EVER COMPLIMENTED A lady on the beautiful dress she is wearing only to hear her say, "This old thing? I've owned it for years." Their response throws water on your good intentions, doesn't it? Mother knew how to receive a compliment. She simply smiled and said thank you. She never said much more except on occasions when you complimented her on a gift. If that was the case she always acknowledged it by telling who gifted her with it. She would then return a compliment in some way. I noticed Mother received lots of compliments. I'm convinced it was because she not only knew how to accept one but was generous in passing them out.

Compliments are not only expressed verbally. They can be given through actions. These deeds can be in silence, accomplished with only a look, smile, or a touch, such as holding someone's hand, hugging them, or just your mere physical presence with no words required. We realize praise many times by the resulting feeling that washes over us. God uses many ways to uplift us. Mother taught that our part is simply be open to recognize which means the Almighty chooses.

I give a very extraordinary example to you. Shortly after Mother's passing a close sister in Christ sent me a sympathy card. But it was not just any sympathy card. I was unaware that years before, when her mother passed away, my mother had handwritten a poem and enclosed it in her sympathy card to my friend. Mother told her she believed these would be the words her mother would say to her. This Christian sister saved this correspondence from Mother down through the years; when my mother died she simply paid it forward by mailing me the very poem in Mother's handwriting. I do not know the author to credit but I share this poem with you:

When I Must Leave You

When I must leave you for a little while
Please do not grieve and shed wild tears
And hug your sorrow to you through the years.

But start out bravely with a gallant smile;
And for my sake and in my name
Live on and do all things the same.
Feed not your loneliness on empty days,

But fill each waking hour in useful ways.
Reach out your hand in comfort and in cheer
And I in turn will comfort you and hold you near;

And never, never be afraid to die,
For I am waiting for you in the sky.

What an encouragement I received from this lady! It was one of comfort and knowing one more time how Mother complimented people in quiet loving ways which spoke louder than any audible words.

Rejection

"Thou shalt not be afraid for the terror by night;
nor the arrow that flieth by day;"
—Psalm 91:5 (KJB)

"So that we may boldly say, The Lord is my helper,
and I will not fear what man shall do unto me."
—Hebrews 13:6 (KJB)

"In righteousness shalt thou be established: thou shalt
be far from oppression; for thou shalt not fear: and
from terror; for it shall not come near thee."
—Isaiah 54:14 (KJB)

"Let nothing be done through strife or vainglory; but in lowliness
of mind let each esteem others better than themselves."
—Phil. 1:6 (KJB)

"Let your conversation be without covetousness; and
be content with such things as ye have: for he hath
said, I will never leave thee, nor forsake thee."
—Hebrews 13:5

"But godliness with contentment is great gain."
—I Timothy 6:6

*"Difficulties are meant to rouse, not discourage. The
human spirit is to grow strong by conflict.*
—William Ellery Channing

R EJECTION IS ONE OF LIFE'S most painful emotions to endure. I am speaking of utter denial of our companionship when it becomes quite clear we are not wanted by another. It is a despicable feeling we never forget. Ironically, I have observed this emotion in what are considered the world's most beautiful, successful, and sought after celebrities. Invariably, when interviewed, the star is asked the age old question, "Were you popular in school?" Many of them can even remember the names of classmates who caused them pain.

Not being accepted for who we really are is one of the deepest insults imaginable. It is probably at the top of the list for reasons we pretend to be something we're not. Everyone wants to be liked. It is a normal desire. Even God recognized this need in the most perfect place on earth, the Garden of Eden, when He created for Adam his companion, Eve. But when someone speaks an aside that even remotely hints of ostracism we resort to blending in with the pack. We do not want to bear banishment from society. I sadly think of many recent news reports where teens have taken their lives due to bullying and rejection. It is a seemingly intolerable emotion.

If you have never lived through the agony of extreme rejection you are blessed. The much repeated phrase "You can please some of the people some of the time, but not all of the people all of the time" is never truer. It is one thing to be the subject of gossip and innuendo. All those who participate in this petty game should never make us, as Mother put it, lose one minute of sleep. Those who love gossip are birds of a feather; they do flock together. If you unintentionally find yourself in their nest, however, here is the best strategy for handling it. I simply say, "I have to spend my time talking to God about *my* life, and that's a full time job. I'll be happy to lift this person up in prayer if you like. I don't have to know all the details because God already knows them."

Nearly every time this response puts a damper on the scuttlebutt. Mother gave me this advice while I was in high school and it works like a charm. Now it is altogether a horse of a different color to actually undergo the pangs of extreme exclusion. The causes can be based on factual truths or lies and deceit. The reasons really matter not. The end result is the same: humiliation, embarrassment, and sorrow. If you ever walk this road in life you will be forced to face the one condition many dread--solitude. So if you have never practiced being alone you will find yourself in great fear. On the other hand, if you are comfortable in your own skin as well as your relationship with God and know the truth of the matter, the terror, the depression, and the loneliness will not overwhelm you.

Do you personally say yes to too many requests in order to be liked and assuage the guilt either of your own conscience or at the hands of the requester? Many times we just want to be popular so we believe traveling down the *yes road* will cause us to arrive at *Well-likedville.*

Life is centered round relationships. If we fail to exercise loving acceptance how can we expect a peaceful existence? This is not to say we are to accept negative or abusive people. What I am saying is, have respect for everyone. Jesus died for all humankind. So if it is good enough for Jesus it should be no less for us. If we accept this simple truth in God's word then the act of receiving changes, compliments, and rejections hinges on acceptance of everyone. Acceptance makes the changes, compliments, and rejection less monumental on a day-to-day basis. The highs aren't so high and the lows aren't so low. We can live daily on a more even keel.

REFLECTION EXERCISES:

1. Who do you most struggle with accepting? Should you sever the relationship or are there enough positive aspects to seek resolution or restoration?
2. What transitions have recently been difficult to accept? Which ones have been easy to accept? How can you focus more on the positive ones?

3. Write down three compliments you've recently received. Read them out loud and hear the acceptance God has given you as you listen to your own voice.

4. For the next seven days speak a compliment to one person you know and one stranger every day.

5. Name a time you felt rejected. Go back and repeat number three.

Here is my beautiful mother at age 74.
Do you see the gleam in her eyes?

CHAPTER 7

Humility

"By humility and the fear of the Lord are riches and honor, and life."
—Prov. 22:4 (KJB)

H UMILITY IS AN AMBIGUOUS WORD in our culture. Perception of its definition varies from person to person. Some individuals believe humility is vastly over rated. Many successful people believe they cannot afford to be humble, while others adhere to a worm mentality. Let's look at the definition of humility: being plain and simply lacking of self- importance.

Susella was considered a woman of great humility because she did not portray self-importance. One of humility's synonyms is meekness. A lot of people equate meekness with weakness. This is far from the truth. Meekness is defined as" easily managed or handled." Mother was very easy to be around, yet at the same time we all saw her as strong and courageous. There are four areas of humility in which Susella Hickey Seals left an indelible mark on me: *talents, blessings, challenges, and choices.*

Talents

"Now there are diversities of gifts, but the same Spirit."
—I Corinthians 12:4 (KJB)

"Having then gifts differing according to
the grace that is given to us…"
—Romans 12:6 (KJB)

"And unto one he gave five talents, to another two, and to
another one; to every man according to his several ability…"
—Matthew 25:15 (KJB) (I understand this is used in
the scripture as a form of money but I believe the same
principle applies to our definition of talents, also.)

W E ALL HAVE BEEN GIFTED with special talents. Just like God's
snowflakes, no two talents are alike. Mother realized right
away I was not too fond of school, but she also picked up on my love
for music. Consequently, I started piano lessons. She told me years later
her rationality was that the piano would make me like school better.
It did! I enjoyed school much better the one day each week I had my
piano class with Mrs. Carden. God blessed me with a gift, and by age
ten I was playing in church.

Mother and Daddy made sure I understood several basic truths
about talents:

1. They carry an important responsibility never to be taken
   lightly.
2. Everyone has a talent but mere humans tend to grade on a

curve. Placing more emphasis on one talent over another simply because a particular gift seems more important is unethical in God's eyes. Certain giftedness places some in front of people while other talents are more behind the scenes. They are all of equal importance.

3. When around someone with a similar talent always put them first, no matter the level of aptitude. That way you don't seem to, as Mother put it, "be full of yourself."

Most everyone has more than one talent, and like many attributes, if honed, can become sharper. Conversely, if gifts are underutilized, the gifts will wane. We can, if found to be good stewards of our innate capabilities, discover new proclivities. (Read more about stewardship in chapter 10.)

Blessings

"Blessed be the Lord, who daily loadeth us with
benefits, even the God of our salvations."
—Psalm 68:19 (KJB)

"Every good gift and every perfect gift is from above,
and cometh down from the Father of lights, with whom
is no variableness, neither shadow of turning."
—James 1:17 (KJB)

*"He has achieved success who has worked well,
laughed often and loved much."*
—Elbert Hubbard

BLESSINGS ARE ALL THE GOOD that God wants to gift us in our lives. Mother always maintained equanimity about those wonderful events I wanted to shout about from the roof top. She explained it something like this: "Well, life's good things mean something different to everyone. A blessing to you might be a new car while a huge blessing to another could be just this month's payment on their five-year-old vehicle."

Once more, Mother's simple way of foraging life's principles were concise and to the point. She reminded me to savor the seasons of good so I could recall them when challenges arose. Of equal importance, Susella emphasized the mercies of everyday benefits which many of us take for granted until they are taken away. (This principle travels well with our chapter on gratitude.)

Blessings can appear in disguise as challenges or trials. We all can look back over times when something as simple as being late for an appointment, which unnerve us, only to discover on down the road that an accident could very well have involved us, had we been running on time. I am reminded of the Garth Brook song, "Thank God for Unanswered Prayers." We all are guilty of praying and wishing for certain things that never materialize. Then, with hindsight being twenty/twenty, we see God really gifting us with a blessing by saying no.

I remember the first time Mother and I discussed Romans 8:28: "For all things work together for good to them who love the Lord and are called according to His purpose." She told me to make sure I noticed the word "all" in this verse. She reminded me that sometimes God allows us to see the why in this life and sometimes we'll only understand in the next life. That's hard to swallow, but once again, being a lover of the old time gospel songs I was raised on, I'll hum or sing "We'll Understand It Better By and By."

Challenges

"Let your light so shine before men, that they may see your good works, and glorify your Father which is in heaven."
—Matthew 5:16 (KJB)

"These things I have spoken unto you, that in me ye might have peace. In the world ye shall have tribulation: but be of good cheer: I have overcome the world."
—John 16:33 (KJB)

"But he giveth more grace. Wherefore he saith, God resisteth the proud, but giveth grace unto the humble."
—James 4:6 (KJB)

"Difficulties are meant to rouse, not discourage. The human spirit is to grow strong by conflict."
—William Ellery Channing

AT FIRST GLANCE ASSIGNING THE word humility alongside the word "challenges" may seem somewhat ill-fitting. You may believe humbleness is all we can ever garner when going through seasons of trials. During times like these we do feel humbled, but often we like to lament our case to anyone who will listen. It is so easy to go into self-pity or martyrdom mode. We want all mankind to feel sorry for us. Somewhere deep in our psyche we believe if everyone can just understand how very bad it is, they will pity us and offer to help. But have you noticed how, if you start sharing your hard times, the other person, more often than not, launches into a litany of every bad situation they've ever experienced? And that somehow those always manage to seem worse than your problems? I am not sure if people are trying to get us to see that what we're experiencing is not nearly as bad as we are making it, or if they never had anyone to vent their struggles to at the time they were experiencing them. In my opinion, it's probably a little of both.

But the bottom line is, no one likes a complainer. It's not necessarily that we see it as complaining. It's just that many times we feel isolated in so many of life's battles. We are convinced we are the only person on earth to ever go through anything quite like this (and sometimes, this is the case). It's me against the world, baby! My mother, however, through daily struggles with her health, served as a true paragon of humility. She never complained even though I knew she was in great pain. Most days when inquiring about how she felt, Mom's answer was nearly always the same —very well. To me this reply spoke volumes to all who observed her. Even when Mother reached the point where she had to arrive at her church pew in a wheelchair she did so with grace and a smile. I've had numerous people in church tell me there were many Sundays when they did not feel like going to church, "but Mrs. Seals would come to mind, and I knew if she could make it to church, then I could too".

Choices

"And thou shalt teach them diligently unto thy children, and shalt talk of them when thou sittest in thine house, and when thou walkest by the way, and when thou liest down, and when thou risest up."
—Deuteronomy 6:7 (KJB)

"I will instruct thee and teach thee in the way which thou shalt go: I will guide thee with mine eye."
—Psalm 32:8 (KJB)

"The meek will be guided in judgment; and the meek will he teach his way."
—Psalm 25:9 (KJB)

"And I will bring the blind by a way that they knew not; I will lead them in paths that they have not known: I will make darkness light before them, and crooked things straight. These things will I do unto them, and not forsake them."
—Isaiah 42:16 (KJB)

"Good judgment comes from experience.
Experience comes from bad judgment."
—Jim Horning

"Destiny is not a matter of chance; it is a matter of choice. It is not a thing to be waited for, it is a thing to be achieved."
—William Jennings Bryan

HUMILITY IN CHOICES – WHAT a concept! It is only our very Adam nature where we make choices by putting one's self first. Observe little babies. Grabby, grabby – they grab everything for themselves. Psychology says one of the initial signs of self-fulfillment is an infant's inclination to put everything in their mouth. It's all about me. Many of us never mature past this point. We think of ourselves first. Now this writer does not believe for one moment we should not treat ourselves kindly. If one is offered blessings of any kind, say, a promotion at work, and believes it is a positive move for their life, by all means, congratulations. It is all a matter of balance. But when we aim for the top of every heap in life out of personal greed and grandiosity, it can sometimes be to our detriment in the long run. All our choices should be made with much forethought and prayer. I am speaking of making choices in life with a spirit of unpretentiousness. Do we think about how the consequence of our choices affect other people in our lives, or is it just all about me?

We all have made poor choices somewhere down life's road. The important rule to remember is accepting responsibility for making wrong choices. Don't put the blame on someone else if we know, in our heart, it is our mistake. If there is a way to right it, do so, promptly. If it has been a choice resulting in irreversible improprieties, ask forgiveness from all involved. But be prepared; you might not receive absolution. Do remember this: the fruit of any wrong choice contains the seed of a lesson to be learned. Discover the lesson, strive to never repeat it, and then move on. Continually dwelling on the failure can sometimes land us in a state of immobility where even the simplest of choices become monumental. If we find ourselves in this position, many times we are in real need of professional help, Godly counsel, or both.

As per the theme of this book, I have a Susella-ism to back these claims. Mother was offered a promotion where she had worked for years. She would work as a supervisor and receive a pay raise. I remember being excited when she shared the news with Daddy and me over the supper table. But then she said that she turned it down. When I asked her why, her gentle answer revealed she had observed that other supervisors went through a lot of added strain and overtime for the added pay. She decided that she preferred to spend her time with us. I never felt deprived in any shape, form, or fashion because Mother made a choice to put her family ahead of any personal recognition, achievements, or extra money.

The fruits of the spirit include humility or meekness as King James calls it. We are easily humbled facing challenges or poor choices. There seems to be someone around every corner who likes to remind us of them. If we're not careful, Satan can deliver us a boatload of guilt. Then, we could spend the rest of our lives rowing upstream with regret. Stop! Ask God for forgiveness by being like Peter and step out of the boat, keeping your eyes fixed on Jesus instead. Learn the lesson, but humbly give praise to the Almighty for His deliverance during times of storms. With this lesson gained, it will prove to be much easier to possess genuine humility in areas of talents and blessings. You will discover a spirit of generosity with your talents and blessings. A gentler side, which was not present before, will display itself. Doors will open for you to share with others lessons you learned during the hard times, if you maintain the same meek attitude during the good times.

REFLECTION EXERCISES:

1. Name your best two talents. Ask friends, if you get stuck.
2. What are your top three blessings? How can you celebrate these with others?
3. List three challenges you are struggling with currently. What options of resolution are available right now? If you wait, could additional options present themselves?
4. Name a poor choice you've made and the result. Name a good choice you've made and the result.

CHAPTER 8

Honor

"He shall call upon me and I will answer him: I will be
with him in trouble; I will deliver him and honor him."
—Psalm 91:15 (KJB)

T HE WORD *HONOR* MEANS HAVING a clear sense of what is morally
right. A second meaning is a feeling of deference, approval, and
liking. When used as a verb honor means "to have a high opinion of, to
pay tribute to, to be recognized or to lend dignity to by an act or favor."
On awakening each morning, we should pay honor to God by thanking
Him for the gift of another day. Many people were not as fortunate as
you and I. It goes back to living in the present. This is all we know for
sure--today. Mother paid particular obeisance to the following four
arenas: *faith, country, little things, and authority.*

If we follow suit, we all can abide in a victorious environment.

Faith

"Now faith is being sure of what we hope for
and certain of what we do not see." '
—Hebrews 11:1 (NIV)

"And without faith it is impossible to please God, because
anyone who comes to him must believe that he exists
and that he rewards those who earnestly seek him."
—Hebrews 11:6 (NIV)

"Let us fix our eyes on Jesus, the author and perfecter of our
faith, who for the joy set before him endured the cross, scorning
its shame, and sat down at the right hand of the throne of
God. Consider him who endured such opposition from sinful
men, so that you will not grow weary and lose heart."
—Hebrews 12:2, 3 (NIV)

"As the body without the spirit is dead, so
faith without deeds is dead."
—James 2:26 (NIV)

"We are not human beings having a spiritual experience.
We are spiritual beings having a human experience."
—Pierre Teilhard de Chardin

GOD'S WORD SAYS IN HEBREW 11:1, "Now faith is the substance of things hoped for, the evidence of things not seen." My everyday interpretation is to believe without seeing. We all express faith in something. Even the lowliest of thinkers has faith in electricity. We all flip the light switch in faith, believing the room will be illuminated. Think in terms of Jesus as the light switch. John 12:46 says, "I am come a light into the world, that whosoever believeth on me should not abide in darkness."

In what or whom do you have faith? Many individuals have faith in their own abilities. Some possess high regard for their education and degrees. Others honor their wealth or social standing, while numbers defer to a particular denomination or church. Do you know what God thinks about this? Read Psalm 118:8: "It is better to trust in the Lord than to put confidence in man." Before paying homage to these worldly acclaims, we must know beyond a shadow of doubt that first and foremost we possess *faith in God*. Why? Because we are told in Hebrews 11:6: "But without faith it is impossible to please him: for he that cometh to God must believe that he is, and that he is a rewarder of them that diligently seek him." We are commanded by God to have faith in Him; otherwise we will never please Him. Neither secular jobs performed nor good Christian works will be enough to warrant Heaven. We must believe in God. We should believe He sent his Son to die in our place for atonement of our sins in order to possess Heaven. Have faith in the One who made you. Acquiesce to the One who knew you *before* you were ever in your mother's womb.

How can I make such a profound statement? Look at Jeremiah 1:5: "*Before (*italics mine*)* I formed thee in the belly I knew thee...." (I wonder if proponents of abortion have any knowledge of this Bible verse). Allow me to simplify further: have faith in God, not yourself. That is always what Mother told me to remember. Proverbs 3:5 reads: "Trust in the Lord with all thine heart; and lean not unto thine own understanding." You have probably heard the term "blind faith." All faith is blind. Faith says we can't see what we believe and our own understanding is oft times on hiatus. This is completely all right. Mother taught me to have faith in Him in these moments and memorize Isaiah 26:3: "Thou wilt keep him in perfect peace, whose mind (*your understanding*) is stayed on thee: because he trusteth in thee." (KJB)

Country

"If my people, which are called by my name, shall humble
themselves, and pray, and seek my face, and turn from their wicked
ways; then will I hear from heaven, and will forgive their sin, and
will heal their land. Now mine eyes shall be open, and mine ears
attend unto the prayer that is made in this place. For now have
I chosen and sanctified this house, that my name may be there
forever: and mine eyes and mine heart shall be there perpetually."
—II Chronicles 7:14-16 (KJB)

"It is not who is right, but what is right, that is of importance."
—Thomas Huxley

MOTHER AND DADDY TAUGHT ME to honor our country. As
children we all learned to recite the Pledge of Allegiance to the
flag. Now as adults about the only time we even say it is at special events
or on patriotic holidays. If you ever get the opportunity, please listen
to a recitation by the late Red Skelton, a very famous comedian of the
50's and 60's and always a favorite of my parents. He gives definition to
each and every word of our pledge of allegiance. You can go on line and
simply enter the words "Red Skelton's Pledge of Allegiance" and listen
to it. It is the best example I have ever heard expressed in honor of our
country. It succinctly defines all the privileges we enjoy as Americans.

We should always show high respect for the country God gave us as
a birthright. It does not necessarily mean we agree with all aspects of our
government and legislation. It does, however, mean we should express
honor for the phenomenon of freely being able to choose to disagree

through voicing our opinions, peaceful demonstrations, the privilege of voting, and other such liberties and benefits. Our blessed nation is not perfect because it is made up of an imperfect society--you and me. But it is the best country on earth. I remind you, though some of you will disdain, our forefathers based our freedoms on honoring God first, then country. Be kind and forgiving toward your country. Honor your nation in ways that speak to you. It may mean flying "Old Glory" from your front porch year round. It could mean writing to servicemen away from home. It might be something as simple as daily praying for our country, as I overheard Mother one precious time in childlike reverence whispering, "Lord thank you for blessing me to be an American. Forgive us all for not noticing everything you do for us. Forgive those who wish us harm. Cause protection and favor to fall over everyone in the United States of America." As usual her words were short, sweet, to the point, and oh so scripturally sound.

Little Things

"Who despises the day of small things?"
—Zechariah 4:10 (NIV)

"Go to the ant, you sluggard consider its ways and be wise."
—Proverbs 6:6 (NIV)

"A little one shall become a thousand, and a small one a
strong nation: I the Lord will hasten it in his time."
—Isaiah 60:22 (KJB)

*"Sometimes when I consider what tremendous consequences come from
little things...I am tempted to think...there are no little things."*
—Ralph Waldo Emerson

GOOD THINGS COME IN SMALL packages. We've heard this all our lives. But do you really believe it? My Daddy was a small man physically, but he still looms large in my life. He always has and he always will. He exuded love for everyone. His life has exemplified God's love not only in my life but many lives in which he came in contact. So, yes, I'm a firm believer in good things coming in small packages.

What about the day to day hum-drum routine of living? Do you get bored easily? As I once did, do you live for those circled dates on your calendar? You know, the special occasions you look forward to: a much anticipated vacation, a promotion, a wedding, party, baptism, graduation, reunion, theater date, concerts, retirement, etc. I cannot tell you the number of people I've heard speak of their lives only in terms of "when I retire." Then there are those who talk about finding true happiness when they marry or have a child. Do they think their lives are meaningless until then? The trouble with this mindset, as Mother reminded me, is we live far more days of ordinariness than we do the red letter days. So can you see the ineffective existence we are creating for ourselves? Mother seemed to live daily with a divine knowledge of how our lives can impact other people in even the smallest ways. I believe that is why she exuded the joy she did in small matters of day-to-day life. There was so much love put into everything she did, whether it was quilting a baby quilt for an expectant mother, babysitting her grandchildren, or simply coordinating Daddy's clothes on Sunday morning for church. She always seemed to be in the moment. She epitomized Ecclesiastes 9:10,11, which I remember her reading aloud to me once: "Whatsoever thy hand findeth to do, do it with thy might; for there is no work, nor device, nor knowledge, nor wisdom, in the grave, whither thou goest. I returned, and saw under the sun, that the race is not to the swift, nor the battle to the strong, neither yet bread to the wise, nor yet riches to men of understanding, nor yet favour to men of skill; but time and chance happeneth to them all." (KJB) Mother taught all those around her how the small common- place joys make up ninety percent of our lives. And if we do not take in these everyday delights, the other ten percent of captivating times will not fill our joy cup for a lifetime of happiness.

Use all of your senses to pay tribute to an average day. Draw in deep breaths of a refreshing spring shower, the smell of a pot roast cooking, or a freshly mowed lawn. Close your eyes and inhale the sweet aroma of a fresh flower; touch the petals and sense their delicacy. Use your sight as if a child again. On a summer day, what shapes do the clouds remind you of when you look at them? What about the time in the store when a stranger paid you a compliment? Didn't your day seem brighter and did you not recall those words for a long time afterwards? When in conversation with another, really listen when that person is talking to you. Look them directly in the eye. Let them know they are the most important person on the face of the earth at that moment in time. If you do these things, you will hear a louder voice coming from their soul than the words coming from their lips.

What is so bad about honoring the small things in life? I guarantee you there will come a day in everyone's life when some of the most trivial and mundane occurrences will revisit your intellect. This time your perspective will be altogether different. The once ordinary will become quite extraordinary. Once you experience one of these reasoning meridians, you will never be the same again. Consequently, honoring the small things in life will become second nature to you. Unfortunately, many of us who learn this lesson have done so through tragedy. Please take it from the voice of experience: Learn to stop and smell the roses.

Susella's life demonstrated how little time it takes to reap great feelings of contentment by bestowing and observing the smallest pleasures. The reason I believe this is, in 1994, Mother was in a Chattanooga hospital recuperating from surgery and I posed this question: "Mother, how do you always remain so quiet even though I know you are in pain?"

Her response went something like this, "Well, honey, it doesn't make the pain go away to moan about it. I just turn it over to the good Lord and trust Him to ease the pain. I remember Jesus suffered for you and me and I'm not better than Him. If He suffered, so I can, too. I know I trust Him with all the big things, so I might as well give him the little things too."

At that moment in time, thinking that her pain was not a "little thing," I felt like the world stood still. It was one of the most profound and simple proclamations I'd ever heard. It touched me on a spiritual level unlike the best Sunday school lesson or sermon from the pulpit. What a testimony! May we all practice Mother's personification of I Timothy 4:12: "Let no man despise thy youth; but be thou an example of the believers, in word, in conversation, in charity, in spirit, in faith, in purity."

So now that we know even the smallest efforts can reap great benefits in others' lives, determine today to go out and impact others in a positive way. We really can make a difference, even in a stranger's life.

Authority

"Woe unto them that decree unrighteous decrees, and
that write grievousness which they have prescribed;"
—Isaiah 10:1 (KJB)

"Likewise, ye husbands, dwell with them according to knowledge,
giving honor unto the wife, as unto the weaker vessel, and as being
heirs together of the grace of life; that your prayers be not hindered."
—I Peter 3:7 (KJB)

"Likewise, ye wives, be in subjection to your own husbands;
that, if any obey not the word, they also may without
the word be won by the conversation of the wives."
—I Peter 3:1 (KJB)

"Children, obey your parents in the Lord: for this is
right. Honor thy father and mother; which is the first
commandment with promise: That it may be well with
thee, and thou mayest live long on the earth."
—Ephesians 6:1-3 (KJB)

"Let as many servants as are under the yoke count
their own masters worthy of all honor, that the name
of God and his doctrine be not blasphemed."
—I Timothy 6:1 (KJB)

"Masters give unto your servants that which is just and
equal; knowing that ye also have a Master in heaven."
—Colossians 4:2 (KJB)

"Feed the flock of God which is among you, taking the oversight thereof, not by constraint, but willingly; not for filthy lucre, but of a ready mind."
—I Peter 5:2 (KJB)

"Obey them that have the rule over you, and submit yourselves: for they watch for your souls, as they that must give account, that they may do it with joy, and not with grief: for that is unprofitable for you."
—Hebrews 13:17 (KJB)

"Render therefore to all their dues: tribute to whom tribute is due; custom to whom custom; fear to whom fear; honor to whom honor."
—Romans 13:7 (KJB)

"In this world man must either be anvil or hammer."
—Henry Wadsworth Longfellow

MANY TIMES WE RESENT THOSE who rule over us. It starts at an early age when we tire of our parents' regulations. Then we are affronted by our employers and co-workers. Let's not even get started on resentments toward our teachers, spouses, siblings, and oh, yes, the government. I imagine this is all a complex part of the inherent free will God fashioned in each of us. It is God's intention, however, for us to render honor to those in authority. It is an important segment of God's ordinances in order for His divine will to be carried out here on earth. He already knows the outcome of each election, whether you believe it or not. ("Let every soul be subject unto the higher powers. For there is not power but of God: the powers that be are ordained of God." Romans 13:1) He knows each judge who will ever be named to each and every court system. Whether or not we agree with their rulings, I am comforted to know what God says about them: "And said to the judges, Take heed what ye do: for ye judge not for man, but for the Lord, who is with you in the judgment." II Chronicles 19:6 (KJB)

All our resentment, complaining and belittling offer no solutions. This attitude only engenders more of the same into our personal lives from those who have to listen to our rancor. We must remind ourselves that the whole of authority will answer to Almighty God come Judgment Day. This is not authority only on the big scale mentioned; parents will answer to their authority over their children, husbands to wives (and vice versa), children to their parents, pastors to their congregations, employers to their employees (and vice versa). The list is long and we must remember that we will not only give an account for our words and actions but even our thoughts. I don't know about you, but that is a very humbling and sobering thought to this woman!

Since honor means to pay tribute to or a clear sense of what is right, honor God by using the measure of faith He has gifted each of us (Roman 12:3). Honor our country by paying tribute in some form to let our Heavenly Father know you are grateful He chose your nation to be founded on Godly principles. Mother and Daddy paid homage by exercising their right to vote. Do you?

Honoring the little things can rest on conceding that you live in a land where you can participate in small, everyday freedoms many around the world consider luxuries. I heard somewhere that if you have any money in the bank, a few bucks in your wallet, and some extra change in a dish in your home, you are wealthier than seventy percent of the world's population. Although we do not always agree with authority, even Jesus gave us a clear cut example of honoring authority in Matthew 22:17-21.

REFLECTION EXERCISES:

1. Where is your faith level? Look up scriptures referring to faith. Write down these verses and keep a faith study. Meditate and pray on a different scripture each day.
2. Do you complain to others about all that is wrong with America? What can you do to honor your country? (write to deployed servicemen, work in a soup kitchen or give to a homeless or women's shelter, etc.)
3. What little things do you take for granted? How can you correct this oversight?
4. Name those who have authority over you. Write a thank you note to one of your authority figures.

This photo was taken some time in 1938 for Estel and Susella's engagement photo. As a young girl, I always thought it was so romantic that Daddy celebrated the anniversary of their engagement as well as their marriage. How many men do you know who does that?

CHAPTER 9

Gratitude

"Giving thanks always for all things unto God and the
Father in the name of our Lord Jesus Christ."
—Ephesians 5:20 (KJB)

A LOT HAS BEEN WRITTEN AND much discussion generated on talk shows about gratitude. We have been encouraged to keep gratitude journals, and there is absolutely nothing wrong with this practice. If this helps you remain in a state of thankfulness, then, but all means, go for it. Mother seemed to keep a spirit of gratitude about her through her words. So many of her statements began with, "I'm just so grateful"; it eventually sank into my pea brain that a lot has to do with the words flying out of our mouths. Between this observation and happening on a book that changed my life, I realized the importance of watching what we say. The "aha" moment came when I read a book in my thirties titled *What You Say Is What You Get* by Don Gossett. I do not know if this book is still in print, but if you can get your hands on it, I feel confident it will be as revolutionary for you as it was for me.

Thankfulness is first a mindset. Then it must be spoken and, if it helps, written down. We live in such a "bigger is better world" that all of us incline only to be thankful for the big things--a new home, a new car, a better job, etc. But after being so heavily influenced by Mother's life, I have come to realize the significance gratitude plays in four specific areas of our lives: *health and healing, sphere of influence, freedom, all things.* These are often either overlooked or taken for granted until no longer present. I've also come to believe that if we make a concerted effort to be ever mindful of these four categories, we will indeed project an air of gratitude whether we are alone or in a crowded room. And people will notice.

Health and Healing

"He sent his word, and healed them, and
delivered them from their destructions."
—Psalm 107:20 (KJB)

"But he was wounded for our transgressions, he was
bruised for our iniquities: the chastisement of our peace
was upon him; and with his stripes we are healed."
—Isaiah 53:5 (KJB)

"And the prayer of faith shall save the sick, and the Lord shall raise
him up; and if he hath committed sins, they shall be forgiven him."
—James 5:15 (KJB)

WHEN I WAS JUST A youngster, Mother would tell me to always thank God for good health. On those many days throughout my life when I experienced excruciating migraine headaches I couldn't quite grasp this concept. That is until one time while accompanying my parents on a hospital visit, I met a young girl who had been diagnosed with a brain tumor. She was in horrible pain and there seemed to be nothing they could give this young girl for relief. But she was in the best mood, though. She just kept telling Mother and Daddy that if this illness was what it took for her father to "get right with the Lord," then she was willing to suffer. I remember crying on the way home, and that night I told Mother I was sorry I had not been more thankful for good health. Yes, the young lady died, but do you know what? Her father gave his life to the Lord. I just know this special lady has a place of honor in Heaven. First and foremost we should all be grateful for the level of health we possess now. Even if there were healthier days in the past, it could be worse in the future, so thank God for your health right here and now.

Secondly, we should be thankful for healing or feeling better. It is really easy to turn to God in prayer with a sincere heart for ourselves or a loved one when we are in the midst of a sickness, accident, or disease. But the minute things take a turn for the better, we forget to thank God for seeing us through, touching our body, or completely and miraculously healing us. There is a story in the Bible about the lepers. Remember there were ten of them, but there was only one who returned to offer thanks to Jesus for healing him (Luke 17:12-19).

Let us always thank God. He can heal us in any fashion He chooses. I recall a time when I received news that, yes, you have cancer. I was beside myself. I remember going home to my lonely apartment in complete and utter despair. I was faithfully attending church and serving God in any way I was asked, and in my mind I just didn't think I deserved this affliction. Thank God for the wonderful Godly counsel I received at that time in my life. I went to the pastor and told him my dilemma. The doctors wanted to admit me immediately the next morning and perform surgery. I had been following the teachings of this Godly minister and studying about healing. I shared with him that I was afraid if I had the surgery I was telling God I didn't think He could miraculously heal me. This spirit filled preacher explained to me that God always meets us at our point of faith. In other words, if I believed God could work through the surgeon to bring about my healing, then I should choose this option. Ultimately having the surgery was my final decision. God honored my faith level and I will forever be grateful for this minister's discerning tutelage.

God has sure seen me through a lot in recent years, but I have also witnessed His mighty hand of healing for others not only physically but financially, spiritually, and in many other areas. As I write these words I am once again facing several personal areas where I could use God's miraculous touch. But observing Mother's faith and courage in God's healing power since that first time I knelt with Daddy and asked God's healing on her has strengthened me greatly. I feel very comfortable praying for others and myself. I thank God for using Mother and Daddy to teach me to pray God's word for healing.

Sphere of Influence

"A good name is rather to be chosen than great riches,
and loving favor rather than silver and gold."
—Proverbs 22:1 (KJB)

"A good name is better than precious ointment….."
—Ecclesiastes 7:1 (KJB)

W E ALL REALLY NEED TO be more cognizant about how powerfully our lives impact others. Believe it or not, we should be thankful for this knowledge. Think back for a moment about a grandparent, parent, teacher, neighbor, pastor, colleague, or friend who immediately comes to mind now that I have broached this topic. Who most influenced you when you were very young? Who influenced your teenage years, your early adulthood? Now think about exactly what that person said or did that affected you? Was it a grandiose statement or action? Many times, the response is no. This is also a plus or minus repercussion.

What do I mean? Recall someone who said something to you that left you miserable. I'll give you an example. Today, years later, I still feel the sting of my second grade teacher's words to my parents at open house: "Let's be glad Sharon is smart. She'll never be an artist." I never let on that I overheard her statement, but it stayed with me. Now fast forward to college. I was taking an art class and part of our final grade was based on creating a painting. In the next to last class session, we had a short written test and then were allowed to start on our artwork. We could then take it home and return the last class meeting with the completed project to receive a final grade. And wouldn't you know it! I was lucky enough to be in a class with a lot of art majors who were outstanding at their craft. Everyone was busy at task while I proceeded to burst into silent tears. All of a sudden, the professor knelt down by me and asked what was wrong. When I told him that, with the combination of all the art majors around me and the memory of the stinging words of my second grade teacher, I just knew I had *failure* flashing brightly above my head. My professor looked at me and said, "I bet you are a water gal, aren't you?"

Surprised, I said as a matter of fact I loved the water and the ocean. He pulled out a half dollar from his pocket, placed it about three-fourths up the canvas and to the right, and penciled a half circle.

"There's your sunset," he said. "Remember your palm trees over to the left to bring some balance like we learned. Now enjoy yourself."

What an impact that had on me. My painting hung at Mother and Daddy's for years and now hangs in my friends Judy and Glen's home. To me, the painting is very primitive, but I did receive a good grade, even though I believe it was partly in sympathy for me. Interestingly, after that art class, when I started work in our local school system many years ago, I walked into the teacher's lounge to discover a water color I had painted in eighth grade hanging there; my teacher had framed it and hung it there for all the other teachers to see. I never knew there was another teacher who thought my art merited such a special place. I share this story to stress the importance of influencing people for good. We never know how potent even seemingly unintended sarcastic remarks can cut deeply into one's emotions.

Please, I admonish you not to be the person remembered for unkind remarks or hurtful actions. We must be ever present in the knowledge of our influence on everyone who crosses our path. Embrace a thankful heart for it. Those people who came to mind earlier, you appreciate what they said or did for you that helped you at the time, right? Then be grateful and pay it forward. Have an appreciative heart towards people. Extend a kind word, possess a giving spirit and a genuine smile. You could be the only one that day who expressed such a considerate disposition to that person. If you were, they will never forget you; your face in their mind's eye will make them smile.

After Mother passed away, I cannot even begin to tell you the number of people who shared their stories of how she made an indelible mark on their lives. Here is just one of those stories. About a year after Mother died, a young lady and I were receiving manicures at our local nail salon. She was talking with her nail tech about her work. I looked at her and told her I didn't understand how she could be working unless it was after school because she looked so young. She laughed and promised me she worked full time at the health facility where Mother spent the last nine months of her life. Just in passing I told her I didn't remember her, but Mother had been a patient there. The young lady asked my mother's name, and when I told her she immediately jumped up and said, "That was the most special woman I have ever met in my life. We all fought over who was going to take care of her. Even when she reached the point where she no longer talked, her eyes could twinkle with more emotion than people who talk. She made me feel so special. May I please have a hug from her daughter?"

Can you imagine how special and deeply comforted I felt at that moment? Never regret sharing even the smallest kind gesture with anyone.

Another more recent family story I must share regarding Mother's influence is about one of my nephews, Steven. He and his wife had a surprise pregnancy after the Lord called Mother home. I remember Mother telling me she had a one-of-a-kind name (her mother had combined the names of her two sisters, Sue and Ella). There would never be another Susella. Well, she was wrong. Her influence was so strong, even after her death, that her eleventh great-grandchild bears her name: Susella.

Freedom

"....Who is on the Lord's side? Let him come unto me...."
—Exodus 32:26 (KJB)

"I call heaven and earth to record this day against you, that
I have set before you life and death, blessing and cursing:
therefore choose life, that both thou and thy seed may live:"
—Deuteronomy 30:19 (KJB)

"...How long halt ye between two opinions? If the Lord
be God, follow him: but if Baal, then follow him...."
—I Kings 18:21 (KJB)

" For God so loved the world, that he gave his only
begotten Son, that whosoever believeth in him
should not perish, but have everlasting life."
—John 3:16 (KJB)

IN THE RECENT YEARS OUR country has not been in good graces with much of the world. Many people wish us great harm. They see us all as a rich, narcissistic body of people. They are right to some degree, but I believe all these nations who abhor us so have some of the same caliber of people in their society as well. The difference lies in our freedoms. Mother and Daddy taught me never to discuss politics and religion in mixed company, so I will not start here.

The point I wish to make, however, is that we are all too lax in being thankful for being born in this country. Whichever side of the political spectrum you reside on is just that--your side, your belief. Just give thanks to the Almighty you are allowed to freely choose. We will never all agree, but this one thing we can know: We live in the greatest nation on earth. Never take for granted that fact. I am encouraged to see more young people getting involved. Let's encourage even more of our youth to put time and prayer into the electoral process. The political scene could, if leaders would so choose, offer a great lesson to our youth in how to resolve differences and come together to effect change for everyone, to build a better world for our children and our children's children.

There is another wonderful freedom bestowed upon us by God himself--the freedom of choice. He does not force us to be a puppet, worship him or believe on his Son, Jesus. He gives us complete freedom to make the choice on our own. My prayer is that you exercise your freedom to choose to believe in Him!

All Things

"Enter into his gates with thanksgiving, and into his courts
with praise: be thankful unto him and bless his name."
—Psalm 100:4 (KJB)

"In everything give thanks for this is the will of
God in Christ Jesus concerning you."
—I Thessalonians 5:18 (NIV)

"And let the peace of God rule in your hearts to the which
also ye are called in one body; and be ye thankful."
—Colossians 3:15 (KJB)

W HEN YOU FIRST READ THIS heading, I bet you flipped back to the beginning of the chapter to make sure you remembered the topic, right? Yes, we're still addressing gratitude. Your first thought is most likely that this is an improbable task: to have gratitude for all things. What about traumas, tragedies, heart breaks? How can anyone ever be thankful for these times? I ask you to think back to the most gut wrenching experience you have gone through up to this point in life. Yes, I know it is hard. Did you learn anything from this time in your life? If the truth be known, we all can confess we learn greater lessons during hard times than we do in good times. A Robert Browning poem says it better than I ever could:

"I walked a mile with pleasure, she chattered all the way.
But left me none the wiser, for all she had to say.
I walked a mile with sorrow, and ne'er a word said she.
But, oh, the things I learned from her, when sorrow walked with me."

The old saying "everyone loves a winner" is never truer. When we're on top, everyone loves us. But let difficulties or a scandal arise and watch the fallout begin. Believe you me, the cream (a true friend) rises to the top during grim times. Having a true friend is one of the most wonderful blessings anyone can be eternally grateful for during any type of difficulty. Mother and Daddy always emphasized that even in the worst of times, there is something positive to be found, be it a genuine friend, a life lesson learned by passing through the fire or flood of a trial, or even something as simple as discovering you really do have more strength than you ever thought possible.

During Mother's last months we whiled away lots of hours I will always treasure. Even though I daily had to watch her suffer, I will never ever regret one moment of time we shared. Before she became completely incapacitated we would talk about anything and everything. I believe Mother never realized just how funny she was. Her humor was one of many charms that captivated her youngest daughter.

During her initial stay at the nursing home she was routinely taken to physical therapy to try and strengthen her. I was told on one particular visit I could see Mother in the rehab area. Upon entering the room I spied Mother in her wheelchair lovingly folding towels. When I asked Mother what she was doing, her quick reply was, "They must be running short on help because they've got me folding their laundry." I lost it and began laughing, and so did Mother; soon others in the room were laughing too, but I know they did not hear the punch line. It was just an atmosphere of love and humor. There are many days, when folding my own towels at home, I relive that precious moment, thank God for it, and begin laughing aloud all over again. (If anyone had ever told me I would smile and laugh while doing laundry, I would never have believed it! Isn't it wonderful how God works that way?)

The point I wish to make about gratitude is it is first a thought process. Remember, the moment we are in right now will never come again. We must be thankful. Some day you will remember reading my admonishment to be thankful. If you read God's word regularly, you will not get very far until you are encouraged to be thankful. It is a wonderful place (feeling gratitude) to be spiritually and mentally. Just as we are pleased when someone says thank you to us, God is pleased when we express thanksgiving to Him. As a matter of fact, I believe He smiles when we thank Him.

A thankful heart is a peaceful heart. Gratefulness for good health often hits home only after we lose it. If you're blessed with good health, thank God right now, for you have the accessibility to operate in a greater capacity in your sphere of influence, your freedoms, and all things in your world. I realize all things are not good things, but physically feeling good can serve as a catalyst when bad things happen.

REFLECTION EXERCISES:

1. When was your last complete physical?
2. Who in your sphere of influence could use some encouragement and gratitude?
3. For what freedom are you most thankful?
4. Name a bad thing which taught you an important lesson and what was the lesson learned?

*This family portrait was taken some time in 1954 – Estel, Susella,
daughter standing, Linda; son, Harold; daughter, Sharon*

CHAPTER 10

Weakness

"My grace is sufficient for thee; for my strength
is made perfect in weakness."
—II Cor. 12:9 (KJB)

OTHER WAS NOT PERFECT. SHE had weaknesses with which she struggled. I admired the way she ultimately dealt with them. From lessons learned through observation of her simple living, I conclude that struggling with weaknesses is a lifetime process. God, in His loving mercy, reveals our shortcomings one step at a time. He walks us through as a way to bring us into greater maturity in relationship with Him and others to fulfill His fundamental purpose for our lives. Here are four issues my mother battled: *physical frailty, timidity, worry, and naivete.*

Physical Frailty

"I can do all things through Christ which strengtheneth me."
—Phil. 4:13 (KJB)

S USELLA WAS STRICKEN WITH RHEUMATIC fever at a very young age. Proper medical care was not available in rural Tennessee in the 1920's. As a result, her heart was permanently damaged. She was frail the rest of her life. Mother told me that as a child she was not allowed to participate in play or some of the outside chores and responsibilities of farm life. She felt like her siblings resented her because of her frailty. Granma Pearl had Mother do inside chores that her two sisters and three brothers thought were not as physically challenging as theirs. They were right. Depression era farming consisted of back breaking work for everyone, including the children. Every family member was expected to make a contribution. Mother's part consisted of basic homemaking duties (i.e. cooking, cleaning and sewing). She helped her mother with family meals. She learned to sew. Her efforts paid off later, for she discovered a passion for sewing and designing her own clothes. I'm convinced these childhood limitations also gave her the impetus to relish her flower garden later in life.

Unfortunately Mother's physical infirmity created friction when she fell in love with Daddy. His family was deeply opposed to their marriage because Daddy was told she probably would not live a long life and having children was totally out of the question. But marry they did, and they produced three children (the beginning of a family that presently consists of thirty-two members), and she lived to the age of eighty-four.

Yes, she was physically frail, but Mother's fortitude and faith in God were a living testimony to *not* always trust human reasoning. God knows all things from the beginning to the end; He always has; He always will. Praise His Holy Name!

Timidity

"I know people see me as backward but I'd rather keep quiet
and appear smart than open my mouth and prove otherwise."
—Susella Seals

"Even a fool when he holdeth his peace is counted wise: and he
that shutteth his lips is esteemed a man of understanding."
—Prov. 17:28 (KJB)

SUSELLA WAS SHY. SHE WAS never one to rattle on like many more
outgoing personalities. I saw her timidity as an admirable virtue.
In her quiet, mild-mannered way people were so comfortable around
her they inevitably confided in her. Backwardness resulted in her not
always having a verbal reply after another's every comment, although
her facial expressions and body language spoke volumes. I've seen her
smile, laugh, and cry, hug, hold a hand, or rub a back soothingly as
only a mother can. When I suffered migraines, she was there to rub my
head, weep empathetically, or hold my hair out of the way as I hung
my head in a toilet.

I asked Mother if she was bashful as a child. She told me she
thought being viewed as a sickly person made her want to withdraw
from everyone. She ended her answer to my question, however, by
adding that she believed her shyness is why God blessed her with
Daddy. She said he was so confident and outgoing. God used Daddy
to draw her out of her shell. God turned one of her weaknesses into
a strength.

Bashfulness affects many people. It can be a result of low self-esteem.

We might not know what causes it, but if you pursue a relationship with one who suffers from timidity, you might find out why. I have been blessed with more than one friendship with a shy person. One person's shyness in particular was the result of a childhood of mental and verbal abuse. There were neither words of encouragement nor demonstrations of affection. This special individual has shared a painful past with me that I know it took courage to reveal. We must realize that many shy people come across as stuck up or give an air that they are better than everyone else, when in fact it is just the opposite. These people in fact are filled with feelings of inadequacy. Sadly, our carnality causes us to make a judgment call based on incorrect information. So, do not make snap decisions; pursue a friendship with a shy person, and you might make a lifelong friend.

Worry

"Take therefore no thought for the morrow: for the
morrow shall take thought for the things of itself..."
—Matt. 6:34 (KJB)

MOTHER GRADUATED MAGNUM CUM LAUDE from Worry
University. She knew worrying was a big weakness for her and
this knowledge bothered her a lot. She told me so: "Worry is not placing
my faith in an all-powerful, all knowing, everywhere God. That's just
plain old sin." She obviously grappled with this flaw most of her life.
Soon after Mother and Daddy moved closer to me, they joined my
home church. I taught an adult Sunday school class and once, after
quizzing me about the next Bible lesson—prayer--Mother surprised
me with her next comment. She asked me if I would lift up a personal
request. I fully expected some type of request for physical healing, but
when I asked her the need she simply responded with tear brimmed
eyes: "worrying."

I was drawn like a magnet to steel to my mother's arms. As we
held each other tightly I prayed right then and there. I can't recall my
exact words, but I'll never forget Mom's first words after saying amen:
"Thank you. I knew the Lord would give you the right words to say. I
feel better."

I can't report that Mother never worried anymore, but in the last five
or six years of her life I didn't hear her use the word "worry" as much. If
she did start to say it in my presence, we exchanged knowing glances.
She would stop in mid-sentence, smile, and rephrase her statement with
words like "faith," "believing," or "trusting." When Mother fell and

broke her hip in 2005 the beginning of her earthly end began. But she never once used the word worry, and I honestly can report I never saw worry on her face.

As a matter of fact my nephew, Donny, and I experienced a mighty work of God while she was in ICU immediately following her hip surgery and the family was told not to expect her to live much longer. During a brief visit Donny and I were on either side of her bed and holding her hand. From within, a glorious smile washed across her face. When we asked what she was smiling about, she replied, "Well, I might as well go out in a blaze of glory!"

My nephew and I withdrew from ICU with tears streaming down our faces. Mother was not worried at all. We are both convinced to this day that she was experiencing the presence of the Divine!

Naivete

"But God hath chosen the foolish things of the world to confound the wise; and God hath chosen the weak things of the world to confound the things which are mighty."
—I Cor. 1:27-29 (KJB)

SUSELLA WAS A NAÏVE PERSON. Her sheltered childhood most likely developed this trait. Before you call me out, please hear my point. Even though *naïve* is defined as free from guile, cunning, or deceit--and that is a wonderful way to be remembered--let me remind you that there is a flip side: Naive also means easily imposed on or tricked. I am happy to report Mom was not by any stretch of the imagination sophisticated in the wiles of the world, and this lack of sophistication made her an easy target. She was quick to believe the best of everyone, but also susceptible to being taken advantage of. Over the years several in our family watched, horror stricken, when a few guileful, cunning people deceived, lied, and exploited her. Many of her loved ones tried to look out for Mama by subtle intervention and education while others chose, out of respect, to protect her through silence. Either choice was emotional for those who loved her. She simply believed what she was told, accepted it as truth, then later suffered pain, regret, and, I'm sure, more than one broken heart. My prayer is the moment this sweet lady was absent from her body and present with the Lord that she received a glorious crown and heard the words, "Well done, my good and faithful servant."

Because of the fall in the Garden of Eden weaknesses are inherent in us all. We struggle with relationships, commit sins, and face challenges. These struggles accompany us throughout life. The Holy Spirit reveals a weak spot, and we pray to receive God's restoration. Then just when we think we've successfully completed a course in growing, the Holy Spirit signs us up for a new class. Why else would it be called the *faith walk?* The apostle Paul, who scripted much of the New Testament, brings this point home in II Corinthians 12:7-10. He tells us he was given a thorn (weakness; something that continually agitates or pricks) in the flesh. After three separate prayers asking God to remove it, Paul accepted God's response to this particular affliction: "My grace is sufficient for thee: for my strength is made perfect in weakness." Let's all learn from Paul's attitude of openness by his response: "Most gladly therefore will I rather glory in my infirmities, that the power of Christ may rest upon me. Therefore I take pleasure in infirmities, in reproaches, in necessities, in persecutions, in distresses for Christ's sake: for when I am weak, than am I strong" (verses 9, 10).

Consider the nugget of truth tucked inside these powerful verses. Should we surrender to God our weaknesses (like Mother's physical frailty, shyness, worry, and gullibility)? I give you a resounding *yes!* What follows is a life filled with confidence and security for Christ's power to rule and reign. Actually all the fruits of the Spirit--love, joy, peace, patience, kindness, gentleness, faithfulness, goodness, and self-control--will begin emerging.

The following are poems written and exchanged between Susella and Estel and discovered after their deaths.

FROM ESTEL TO SUSELLA:

Darling your companionship means all the world to me.
Each moment at your side becomes a loving memory.
I like to listen to your voice and every word you say,
Beneath the moonlight and the stars or sunshine through the day.
And whether wind and rain and hail are lashing at the door;
Your closeness is my comfort and I love you even more...
If that is possible dear and considering that you
Are mine to have and hold and I have promised to be true.
Companionship in marriage is the dearest thing in life.
Who knows it better dear than we as husband and as wife.

From Susella to Estel:

Hold on to my hand till we get to the end, for I feel safe with you;
You have always been here for me, and when you go I want to go, too.
We have traveled so many miles together, and had so many hardships
*   along the way;*
But God has a better place awaiting us, when we come to the end of
*   the day.*
I want to be laid to rest beside you, where I've been for so many years.
It is then we will be together forever, never to shed any more tears.

Reflection Exercises:

1. Do you really have faith God can change you?
2. Have you truly believed on Jesus Christ as your Savior? If not, will you do so now?
3. Have you asked Jesus Christ to be your Lord and Master? If not, do so now.
4. Are there any unconfessed sins in your life? If yes, pray and ask forgiveness now.
5. Ask the Holy Spirit to reveal any strongholds where Satan could be hindering your faith walk.

We kids tried to go "all out" for Mother and Daddy's 50th wedding anniversary. There were lots of family, friends and well-wishers who attended. Mother designed and made her dress.

CHAPTER 11

Stewardship

"Who then is that faithful and wise steward, whom
his Lord shall make ruler over his household, to give
them their portion of meat in due season?"
—Luke 12:42 (KJB)

A STEWARD IS AN ADMINISTRATOR OR overseer. The word originally comes from Old English indicating a chiefly historical officer of the royal household who is the administrator over the crown jewels. With this as the original meaning in mind, can you understand the subtle significance of the role we play in overseeing our own lives? We are the administrator over the richest and most important royalty of all--ourselves! If we could all embrace this principle of management of our own lives and less on keeping up with the Joneses, our own crown jewels could be sparkling. Through my research while writing this book, I now see clearly why I always walked a little taller when in the presence of my mother. She was my royalty, my queen. I always thought as a little girl that all Mother lacked was a crown because, as I mentioned previously, when Mother walked into a room it was if royalty had entered. People took notice of her. Hers was never an entrance of pretentiousness, but rather like a breath of fresh air blown into a staid and stuffy room. Everyone seemed to breathe easier. I always noticed all the smiling faces. Based on my observations of Mother, the four most important jewels of her stewardship crown—*time, finances, earth, and heritage*--caused all other jewels in what I'm sure is her heavenly crown to sparkle just as brightly.

Time

"For he saith, I have heard thee in a time accepted…
behold now is the accepted time…"
—II Cor. 6:2 (KJB)

W E'VE ALL HEARD THE OLD adage that "time is money." Well, Mother never equated time with money. Her preference was to view time as a gift, something freely bestowed. Mother valued time as a gracious present from the Almighty. She expressed her genuine thankfulness by carefully redeeming her time while here on earth. Even when she chose to stop physical tasks, either for her household or others, I noticed Mother was mentally enriching her time by reading her Bible, beautiful poetry, a book, or writing down her own thoughts. Her television viewing was a small percentage of her time compared to the rest of us. But I will share one story with you regarding television. Back in the late nineties Mama told me she had discovered a young, new fresh faced preacher on television. She told me she wished I would watch him sometime because she believed he was a sincere person and God was really going to bless him. Wow! Mother sure prophesied correctly on that one. If I were to mention his name, probably all of you would recognize him. Mother's observations regarding this man caused my husband and me to begin listening to his messages; to this day I feel close to Mother each time I watch his program.

Mother believed tithing her time was as important as any other blessing from God. I remember one Saturday night from childhood when she and Daddy were preparing for the next day's worship service.

Mother had just put the finishing touches on her Sunday school lesson and was in the kitchen baking the unleavened bread and washing the paraphernalia to be used in our church's observance of Communion, or the Lord's Supper. (Yes, this was before the era of store bought flatbread and throw away communion cups.) I remember asking her, "Don't you get tired of always being the one who has to do all this?"

"Why, no," she replied. "The Lord is the one who has given me this privilege, not the church, and I should always give my time to the Lord, just like your daddy, and this is one of my ways of doing that."

How could I argue with that? Mother had a penchant for answering all my questions with a simple common sense approach that was always based on Godly principles backed up by scriptures. Then, if you disagreed, Mother would quip amusingly, "You'll have to take it up with your heavenly Father, not me"

Finances

"But thou shalt remember the Lord thy God: for it
is He that giveth thee power to get wealth."
—Deuteronomy 8:18 (KJB)

"Then beware lest thou forget the Lord, which brought thee
forth out of the land of Egypt, from the house of bondage."
—Deut. 6:12 (KJB)

*"Whatever one possesses becomes of double value when
we have the opportunity of sharing it with others."*
—Bouilly

L IVING AS A GOOD STEWARD of our finances is a high calling, indeed. We are bombarded with the commercialism of having more and more. The problem is not necessarily the essence of materialism (although, in and of itself, it presents a prodigious set of difficulties). The stumbling block many times is simply not living in the *now,* as we discussed earlier. We refer to this obstacle in our society as *credit.* Let's correctly identify credit: it is a lifestyle. If we do not have the money for the purchase today, we borrow from tomorrow to have it now. It is, esoterically speaking, stealing from tomorrow.

Yes, of course we all use credit to some extent, but living a way of life using nothing but future earnings places us completely in bondage. No wonder we have to take sleeping pills and are tense, stressed, and sick. No wonder we are unable to have peace and joy in the present because we worry about being able to work in the future to pay for our happiness now. Can you possibly see the futility in all this? What happened to the practice of living within our means? If we could only remember that our Heavenly Father is our provider *(Jehovah Jirah)* instead of ourselves, the economic naysayers would not cause us such personal financial panic.

I observed my parents' practice of the scriptural term tithing. The term plainly means "one-tenth." Most all Christianity advocate this practice. I, like my parents, however, believe the scriptural counsel: "Every man according as he purposeth in his heart, so let him give; not grudgingly, or of necessity: for God loveth a cheerful giver." II Corinthians 9:7 (KJB).

How do you purpose your giving? Give what you do give with a cheerful heart. But if you do not return a tenth, read these words: "Will a man rob God? Yet ye have robbed me. But ye say, wherein have we robbed thee? In tithes and offerings.Ye are cursed with a curse: for ye have robbed me, even this whole nation." Malachi 3:8, 9 (KJB). Do you feel like your life is cursed? Do you want the curse removed? Then the answer is in the next two verses: "Bring ye all the tithes into the storehouse, that there may be meat in mine house, and prove me now herewith, saith the Lord of hosts, if I will not open you the windows of heaven, and pour you out a blessing, that there shall not be room enough to receive it. And I will rebuke the devourer for your sakes, and he shall not destroy the fruits of your ground; neither shall your vine cast her fruit before the time in the field, saith the Lord of hosts. And all nations shall call you blessed; for ye shall be a delightsome land, saith the Lord of hosts." Malachi 3:10-12. Talk about a scripture with *promise!* But every scripture stating a promise also contains a requirement on our part; there is a cause and effect principle in God's word. If we want God to provide the promise, we must be faithful to fulfill our part, our obligation.

Earth

"The earth is the Lord's and the fullness thereof;
the world, and they that dwell therein."
—Psalm 24:1 (KJB)

*"The reasonable man adapts himself to the world: the
unreasonable man persists in trying to adapt the world to himself.
Therefore, all progress depends on the unreasonable man."*
—*George Bernard Shaw*

TOGETHER, MOTHER AND DADDY TENDERLY cared for their piece of earth. Daddy would toil diligently in their vegetable garden at the end of an already hard day's work. Mother's passion for her flowers showed because she lovingly tended them, especially her roses, in a "green" manner. Rather than buying chemical pesticides, she mindfully treated her roses with banana peels and leftover coffee grounds, thus replenishing the soil with potassium. These are just a couple of examples of the myriad of "watch guards" my parents vigilantly put into practice over their Garden of Eden. Mom told me these were the ways Depression-era folks adapted to daily living through re-purposing and reusing household items, because they couldn't afford to do otherwise. Isn't it ironic how our recent economic woes have reintroduced this trend of living? History seems to prove that any time our nation prospers we relegate God's intended essentials for us to the back burner in favor of convenience and sloth. Then we have to learn the lesson all over again.

"The earth is the Lord's and the fullness thereof" is a powerful biblical statement if you think about it. God is the ever omnipresent, omnipotent One who can heal all the ills of our resplendent planet, but from the beginning He intended humankind to have dominion (Genesis 1:28). Why else would he have entrusted Adam the privilege of naming every living creature (Genesis 2:19)? God created the earth for our enjoyment, His gift to us while we live here. Likewise, He has charged us to tend to our little corner of earth in an astute, responsible manner. In an era of political correctness it is called "living green." I respectfully submit it is merely being a faithful steward of God's good earth. Yes, His word tells us that one day He will create a new heaven and a new earth; but let's not be part of the reason why He has to do so sooner rather than later.

Heritage

"Her children arise and call her blessed; her husband also, and he praises her. Many women do noble things, but you surpass them all. Charm is deceptive, and beauty is fleeting; but a woman who fears the Lord is to be praised. Give her the reward she has earned, and let her works bring her praise at the city gate."
—Proverbs 31:28-31 (KJB)

"The greatest thing about man is his ability to transcend himself, his ancestry and his environment and to become what he dreams of being."
—Tully C. Knoles

T HE DEFINITION OF *HERITAGE* IS something immaterial, as a style or philosophy that is passed from one generation to another. One of heritage's synonyms is *legacy* (thus the title of this book).

For what do you want to be remembered? If you were fortunate to enjoy the relationship of family, what one memory first comes to mind when you think of them? What stands out in memory of times with parents, grandparents, aunts, uncles, cousins? Obviously these can be negative or positive influences. If, in your family, there are more negative memories than positive ones, then who is to say it has to be a biological relative who provides you with your legacy? Make conscious efforts to choose positive role models and, for heaven's sake, keep tabs on your children and grandchildren's role models. I read somewhere that friends are the family you choose; so choose wisely!

James, my husband, and I have a god-daughter, Lena; a great-niece, Kayla; and a great-nephew, Bryce. They each call us PePop and Mimi.

They have great relationships with all their grandparents, and we will never take these special people's places in their lives. Do you think for one moment we mind the special names of endearment they use with us? Of course we don't. We feel like they have placed crowns of honor on our heads when their voices sing out those names; we feel special. We have other great nephews and great nieces, but we have not been blessed to be around them as much as we'd like; perhaps someday that will change.

Are you making those around you feel special? Just as a woman exits a room and leaves a slight hint of her perfume, do you leave a path of sweet odors in the form of a smile, a thank you, or a compliment? Whether we realize it or not, our lives are influencing everyone who crosses our path. It can be a family member who walks many years down life's road with us; it can also be a complete stranger who never speaks a word but offers a sympathetic smile as we exchange glances while stopped in a traffic jam. There will be friendships of short duration as well as those, thank God, lasting a lifetime. Accept them all as part of your heritage. These traditions are, as penned in one of Dolly Parton's famous songs, "A Coat of Many Colors."

Remember that God created this earth first, then created us to be good stewards of it. That was his original plan until the Fall. Even after man's disobedience brought a curse our Heavenly Father knew beforehand He would supply the Redeemer to restore both us and the earth. He loves us so mightily that one day He will even create a new heaven and earth for us to enjoy. If we really believe this is to be our future reality, why would we not want to praise our Creator by being more responsible stewards of the present earth? Our task is to practice focused mindfulness to our time and money. In turn, we generate a positive heritage for those who come after us. Being an attentive steward of lifestyles and traditions we pass on to the next generation is a very powerful role, a great responsibility. In fact, if you are faithful to the task, someday someone just might share your legacy with the world.

With all my love and honor, I thank you, Mother, for your legacy.

REFLECTION EXERCISES:

1. What consumes the biggest portion of your free time? Do you believe God is pleased with your answer?
2. Have you ever kept a time journal? If not, try it for one week.
3. What consumes the biggest portion of your budget? Is God pleased with your response?
4. How do you think God would respond to the stewardship of your piece of earth?
5. What legacy are you leaving? Are you pleased or would you like to change it?

After Mother's death I discovered her book of memories. One of the questions was 'Who in the entertainment field do you most admire?' Her answer: Roy Acuff. How appropriate we had taken this picture backstage at the Grand Ole Opry years before.

Epilogue

After having completed this manuscript, I have decided, after much prayer, to add an epilogue that is a vital part to my mother's heritage. From the beginning I chose not to reveal certain family matters because I know there are probably several members of the family who do not know something that Mother and Daddy shared with me many years ago. As I have mentioned throughout the story of my family, some things were never talked about. However, I believe the time has come to break that generational curse because much healing could be realized not only for my family but for anyone who reads this book. It could prove to be a way to reach many women who may be struggling with any life changing decision, so I pray God will use my choice to share this private moment between Mother and Daddy some 50 years ago.

Remember that I said earlier in this book that my parents had no plans for more children after God blessed them with my sister and brother. When Mother found out she was pregnant for a third time, she and Daddy faced a dilemma. First, Mother had the rarest blood type, AB negative. Daddy's blood type did not match. This result of such a mismatch is a condition called the RH factor. Medical history and percentages have shown that a third birth precipitously raises the chances for a Down's Syndrome child.

Second, since Mother had suffered untreated rheumatic fever as a child, she had been advised to bear no children, but she gave birth to two children anyway and suffered from severe damage to her heart. Therefore, no doctor in the rural area we lived wanted her as a patient. She was referred to a specialist in Chattanooga. This doctor sadly informed my parents that Susella would not live to birth a third child, and that this child would have only a 50-50 chance of surviving. The doctor's recommendation was to abort the fetus! His advice was way before the term "therapeutic abortion" had been coined that we hear today.

My parents told me in a rare moment of candor many years later that there was never one minute's hesitation about their decision: They were putting their faith in an Almighty God to see them through. So, Mother was put on bed rest for the remainder of her pregnancy and you, by now, as Paul Harvey use to say, know the rest of the story. I truly believe God entrusted this special couple as my parents because He knew what their decision would be. They would make every effort to ensure that I came into the world healthy and free of disability.

I'm not sure what Mother and Daddy told my sister and brother because you must remember my siblings were at very vulnerable ages (12 and 11) when I was born. For sure, my parents did not tell Linda and Harold of the dangers because they did not want to scare their two beloved children. But I do know my sister and brother had to have sensed something because children are much smarter than we give them credit. My prayer is that any childhood fears or resentments they may have experienced as a result of my birth are forgiven towards Mother, Daddy, and me.

Finally, I just know this book is part of my God-given life's destiny - to share the story of Mother and Daddy's example of sacrifice, unselfishness, and love for not only our family and acquaintances but all who read this. And, to help us remember that all choices we make have consequences. These choices and consequences can often reverberate long past our earthly lives. I wish you peace.

Editor's Note

I have edited a few books over the years, and read even more. But I have never encountered a book like this one. It is rare to find a story told with such sincerity and emotion. Sharon Tate is definitely the product of two exceptional, loving parents who reared her in an atmosphere of love, charity, and a deep reverence for God. No parent in this world could hope to do more.

Above all, this book is the story of one woman's profound influence on her youngest daughter. Susella will live as long as her daughter, Sharon, and her other children as well. She will continue to live through their children; the line is endless. In these brothers and sisters we will always see a portrait of their father, but especially their mother. One day, when all God's children are gathered around that great banquet table in Christ's kingdom, I will count it a privilege to meet this extraordinary woman face to face.

William Fisk, Instructor in English
Tennessee Tech University
February 2013